Lectionary-Based Catechesis for Children

A Catechist's Guide

Sylvia DeVillers

PAULIST PRESS
New York and Mahwah, N.J.

Library of Congress Cataloging-in-Publication Data

DeVillers, Sylvia, 1934–
    Lectionary-based catechesis for children : a catechist's guide/
Sylvia DeVillers.
        p.   cm.
    Includes bibliographical references.
    ISBN 0-8091-3505-1 (pbk.)
    1. Christian education of children. 2. Catholic Church—Liturgy.
3. Lectionaries. 4. Catholic Church—Education. I. Title.
BX926.D49   1994
268′.432—dc20   94-21261
                                                                        CIP

Published by Paulist Press
997 Macarthur Boulevard
Mahwah, New Jersey 07430

Printed and bound in the
United States of America

Contents

Introduction

Lectionary-based catechesis just kind of sneaked up on me one day. There I was happily going about my normal catechetical business, tending to the formation of parish catechists who would be presenting their usual thirty weeks of grade-level religious education and helping Catholic school teachers to create and discover new ideas for their religion classes. I was full of how-to's: how to choose children's texts, how to deal with classroom management problems, how to motivate parents to attend sacrament preparation meetings, how to recruit volunteer catechists, how to find ways to entice the pastor to participate willingly and creatively in religious education programs. The how-to's consumed my energies and filled my days.

And then, when I least expected it, I happened to look behind me, and there, lurking in the shadows like a shy child waiting to be invited to play, I discovered something new to deal with. Lectionary-based catechesis, it seemed, popped up out of nowhere and began quietly to take over where traditional, curriculum-based catechesis left off. I had two choices: ignore it and hope it would go play somewhere else, or learn about it, discover its mysterious attraction, and allow it to join in the fun. I chose to learn all I could, and my search has been rewarded not only with new insight into a rich new catechetical experience but by my own personal growth in understanding of the power of scripture to catechize.

Lectionary-based catechesis has become the buzz word of the Catholic catechetical world of the 1990's. Parish DRE's, Catholic school principals, pastors, diocesan staffs, liturgists, those involved in the order of Christian initiation, and even some parents are looking at lectionary-based catechesis as a means of bringing about renewed enthusiasm for the handing on—and receiving—of the Catholic Christian faith tradition.

Just what is this newest approach to catechesis? Does lectionary-based catechesis indeed deserve the attention it is receiving? Is lectionary-based catechesis a cure-all for the many ills of poorly designed programs of religious education of the past, as some claim? Or is lectionary-based catechesis just one more trendy attempt to hand on the truths of our faith to today's children (and to some adults), doomed to fail in a race "back to the basics"?

Christian Initiation of Children Who Have Reached Catechetical Age

By definition, lectionary-based catechesis is exactly what its title implies: a form of catechetical instruction that refers to and uses the Sunday lectionary readings for its content and methodology. There are, of course, many ways to incorporate the Sunday scripture readings into catechetical programs for children, and some creative catechists have been doing this for as long as there have been people to catechize.

However, lectionary-based catechesis for children, with its emphasis on the Liturgy of the Word, has been used in recent years primarily to prepare unbaptized and/or uncatechized children of a catechetical age for the sacraments of initiation. Since 1988 when the *Rite of Christian Initiation of Adults* was mandated for implementation, the process surrounding these liturgical rites has been the normative way of bringing adults to the sacraments of baptism, confirmation, and eucharist. The same document included adaptations to be used for Christian Initiation of Children Who Have Reached a Catechetical Age (*RCIA,* Part II, #252ff). Now children of a catechetical age are being initiated using a process based on the adult model, and many parishes are suddenly becoming aware of the impact of the Liturgy of the Word on the faith life of these uninitiated children and of the catechetical opportunities to be discovered within the lectionary readings. It was a logical progression that parish children who had been initiated in a traditional manner through infant baptism and first eucharist could benefit from a similar experience.

The Liturgy of the Word for Children

For children in these parishes, the Liturgy of the Word is celebrated and ritualized at a level of understanding appropriate for their ages, developmental capabilities, and spiritual needs. There is the expectation that catechesis (growth in faith) will naturally flow from this ritual as the Word just proclaimed is examined, explained, and connected to the life experiences of the children within the context of a homiletic experience. When

coupled with the entire Sunday liturgical celebration that includes participation with their families in the Liturgy of the Eucharist and surrounded by
their parish faith community, the Liturgy of the Word for children seems to
be an ideal way to hand on the faith of the worshiping community through
participation in the liturgical ritual and celebration. Indeed, the Liturgy of
the Word for children is regarded by some as the most total and complete
way to present the teachings of the Catholic Christian faith tradition.

The objections to this view are many, as we will discover further on
in this book. Liturgists, for instance, caution that the Liturgy of the
Word not be perceived as an experience of catechesis but rather as a
continuation of the liturgical celebration out of which liturgy and
catechesis can come together. Liturgy of the Word, they insist, is a
liturgical experience, not a catechetical one. Intentional catechesis cannot be the primary purpose of the celebration of the Liturgy of the Word
for children: the experience of worship and prayer is the intention.

Parish-Centered Lectionary-Based Catechesis

But because of this renewed interest in the Liturgy of the Word, the
lectionary is often being appropriated as a major source of content for
catechesis, not only in the process of initiating children, but in other
catechetical processes as well.

In its purest form lectionary-based catechesis for children is complicated, multifaceted, and reflects many of the most appealing aspects of
both liturgy and catechesis. In the best of all catechetical worlds, there is a
combination of the liturgical and the catechetical dimensions of parish life
that work together to enhance the faith life of the entire community, adults
as well as children. In this world, the Liturgy of the Word for children is
celebrated by all of the parish children every week throughout the year.
Further response and catechesis based on the Sunday lectionary readings
are offered in additional catechetical sessions in the school, in the homes,
in religious education programs, in small intentional communities, or in all
of the above. Children and adults preparing for the sacraments of baptism,
confirmation, and eucharist through the process surrounding the *Rite of
Christian Initiation of Adults* are catechized during the period of the catechumenate using the lectionary readings as the basis for determining content. Mystagogia is lifelong in this ideal catechetical world, and the formal
catechesis that is developed to answer mature theological questions ultimately leads to a response that results in mission and service.

In that ideal world, adult scripture programs based on the Sunday
readings are included among the normal parish activities, and these

adults are the core out of which scripture shapes the entire parish community. Parish life is influenced by the liturgical seasons which flow into and out of the Sunday liturgy, adding a scripture-based dimension of faith awareness to the community formed by the word of God as it worships together. Indeed, as scripture, liturgy and catechesis come together in this ideal parish, a lectionary-based catechesis which includes both formal content and the celebration of Liturgy of the Word for children is certainly a reasonable approach.

Adaptations of Lectionary-Based Catechesis and the Liturgy of the Word for Children

In its less-than-pure form, however, lectionary-based catechesis can in many ways be seen as a model of adaptation of the human species to its environment. Noting the attention this new venture has received, some intergenerational and family-centered programs focusing on the lectionary have appeared and traditional religious education programs have been developed and adapted using the lectionary readings for their basic content. The adaptations are to be expected, of course, as parish catechetical leaders become more aware of the lack of impact traditional curriculum-based religious education programs seem to have on the faith life of children.

One adaptation involves the insertion of the Sunday lectionary readings as a "prayer experience" at the beginning or the end of the traditional catechetical sessions in both schools and parish religious education programs. While somewhat commendable, this model disconnects the lectionary readings from the rest of the catechetical session and is likely to result in a certain confusion of ideas. In another classroom model the Sunday lectionary readings are used as the basis for some catechesis, to be sure, but the liturgical connection can be missing within the classroom setting.

One lectionary-based adaptation of curriculum-based catechetical programs that is becoming increasingly popular is one in which the lectionary readings are indeed the basis for designing the curriculum for each grade level. The authors of some of these children's texts determine the content of each catechetial session by using whatever "theme" that seems to emerge from the Sunday readings as the topic for catechesis. The authors then design traditional lessons and learning activities according to this theme.

A new sales opportunity has resulted in an abundance of these publications geared to presenting lectionary-based catechesis for children. A few publishers of curriculum-based religious education materials quickly entered the market, offering traditional texts adapted for lectionary-based use. Other long-standing publishers have completely revised their curriculum and texts to reflect interest and enthusiasm for this most recent catechetical phenomenon. Many innovative and original publications and materials including pamphlet-style, loose-leaf format, family "at home" activities, music, videos, and colorful "Bible Storybook" art projects sprouted up seemingly overnight as creative religious educators recognized the appeal of using the Sunday scripture readings as the basis for catechetical programs.

The Liturgy of the Word for children has also been adapted to conform to the logistical or imaginative limitations of parish life. Often these adaptations lack consistency and continuity. This occurs when the Liturgy of the Word for children is presented only occasionally, never on holy days or in the summer, for just those parish children who happen to be attending the Mass at which it is offered, or for very young children who are sometimes perceived as being troublesome or "in the way" at Mass. When there is little attempt to present the Liturgy of the Word for children in a serious and dedicated way and as part of the parish liturgical priorities, it loses some of its effectiveness and therefore some of its liturgical power.

Needless to say, these various adaptations recognize the potential for good that both the Liturgy of the Word for children and lectionary-based catechesis have demonstrated. But these adaptations are limited in their ability to achieve the primary goals of both the Liturgy of the Word for children and lectionary-based catechesis: to discover, celebrate, examine, and share the mysteries of faith as they are expressed within the liturgical experience of the people of God.

This is not to say that some of the various adaptations cannot be useful and good. To the contrary, these adaptations can often lead to much greater freedom to meet the pastoral needs of individual parish situations than rigid adherence to principles. Lectionary-based catechesis is in itself an effective example of a way in which catechetical adaptations become new opportunities for faith to grow and mature. There are many questions and concerns, however, that surround the implementation of lectionary-based catechesis.

Some Issues and Concerns

There is no doubt that lectionary-based catechesis has taken the religious education world by storm. There remain, however, some sober and serious considerations about the most effective and appropriate ways to implement lectionary-based catechesis for children in parish schools and catechetical programs.

There is concern that lectionary-based catechesis is an inadequate tool for presenting the entire body of Roman Catholic doctrine. A major concern for many who are examining lectionary-based catechesis is that doctrinal content will be weakened in programs of religious education which focus exclusively on the Sunday readings. In traditional religious education programs based on a curriculum using scope-and-sequence charts and textbooks, it is clear that important doctrinal elements are presented in a systematic order throughout the school year. The essential doctrinal themes, or "contents" of the lessons, are developed for each grade with increasingly complex and age-appropriate explanations and activities. In the exclusive use of lectionary-based catechesis there is concern that methodology would be repetitious, unimaginative, and would not respect the developmental level of the child. There is concern that catechists would be unequal to the task of interpreting and teaching the Bible. There is concern that a kind of Catholic fundamentalism would spread as more Catholics became familiar with biblical passages. There is concern that too liberal interpretations of scripture would result in watered-down and unfocused theology. These issues and concerns will be addressed in some detail in later chapters of this book as we consider the question of the value of lectionary-based catechesis in contemporary programs of religious education. It is clear, however, that lectionary-based catechesis even in its many adapted forms is becoming an increasingly insistent voice in the catechetical world, and it is important to listen to that voice.

The Role of the Catechist in Combining Curriculum-Based and Lectionary-Based Catechesis

This book maintains that traditional curriculum-based catechetical programs can be enhanced by lectionary-based catechesis and that lectionary-based catechesis needs the basic structure of a traditional program. There are inadequacies in both approaches: when combined in a cohesive way, many of the inadequacies can be overcome. This book offers some suggestions for the successful appropriation of the best and most creative aspects of the recent lectionary-based approach to catechesis while retaining the best and most creative aspects of the more traditional and familiar approach based on curriculum and the developmental needs of children. This combination of curriculum-based catechesis and lectionary-based catechesis will enable children to grow into the faith of the community not only through the process of religious instruction but also through the experience of the parish liturgical celebration.

This book, then, presents a method that combines the two approaches, lectionary-based catechesis and curriculum-based catechesis. The book suggests that traditional catechesis as we know it today is not as effective as we would like in bringing children to maturity of faith, primarily because of a "missing liturgical link," a lack of connection between the catechetical session and the parish Sunday liturgical celebration. In this unitive or combined method, children are encouraged to call to mind the stories of faith that are proclaimed at mass when they participate in the catechetical session. The catechetical session, taken directly from the published curriculum, is chosen to connect with the lectionary readings.

The success of this approach is almost completely dependent upon the formation of scripturally literate, liturgically sensitive catechists. As in all catechetical processes, catechists are always the most vital and important component in bringing people to maturity of faith. This "guide for catechists" is intended for their use, under the guidance of their DRE's, school principals, or other parish catechetical leaders.

It is the intention of this book to help catechists understand how a combined or unitive approach to lectionary-based catechesis can have a far-reaching affect on the quality of catechesis today. Sacred scripture, combined with sound catechetical methodology, can be trusted as the most profound way to discover something about what God is like. Sacred scripture, studied and prayed over the course of the liturgical cycles and combined with sound catechetical methodology, can indeed provide students with a lived understanding of the faith tradition being offered to them. Sacred scripture, as the most vital and profound source of faith, becomes the core out of which can emerge real conversion and formation.

The combined or unitive approach to lectionary-based catechesis provides catechists with the skills and tools necessary to indeed utilize the catechetical method while presenting sacred scripture as the major component of each catechetical session. To do this effectively, catechists must of course be formed in their own understanding of both catechetical methodology and of some basic concepts for interpreting and clarifying the meaning of scripture. This book, as a guide for catechists, attempts to present some ways in which catechists can be strengthened in their ability to understand scripture and to enable them to express that understanding through an effective catechetical process.

Certainly the formation of scripturally-sensitive catechists will aid in the formation of children whose faith is centered on God's word. But primarily it is the faith of the catechist that must be addressed in lectionary-based catechesis as in all catechetical programs. Catechists who experience

God's presence in their lives through scripture will share that experience with those they catechize. A love for God's word will permeate their lives and this love will in turn affect all that they do with the children in their care. This is not, of course, to say that scripture is the only or exclusive aspect of tradition that the catechist will hand on. But catechists for whom scripture is a living expression and source of God's action in their lives will be formed in a basic outlook or attitude of faith that will almost certainly be essential in the transformation of those they catechize.

In the integrative approach proposed by this book, catechists who have been formed in their own faith by their understanding and love of scripture can learn how to discover basic "content" themes within the sacred scriptures proclaimed at Sunday liturgy each week. These themes are then matched with similar themes that are presented in the curriculum-based materials used by the catechist. In planning each catechetical session, the catechist integrates the lectionary readings with the curriculum-based lesson. Thus the catechist makes the vital connection between the Sunday readings and the curriculum-based material, bringing together the best of both approaches. This integrative methodology can result in the children experiencing a sense of connection between what goes on in the classroom and what goes on at Sunday Mass. For them, the catechetical session becomes an extension of their family and parish worship celebration.

In an attempt to move toward the goal of integrating lectionary-based catechesis with traditional catechetical programs it will be important to recognize that neither approach is absolutely perfect and neither approach is totally deficient. There is certainly much to be said about the effectiveness and ineffectiveness of both approaches. But by combining the best of both, a certain catechetical wholeness can be achieved, as the Word becomes alive in the learning experiences of the children who come to us. Catechists who work toward this wholeness by bringing together the Sunday readings and traditional content areas may find themselves among the "models for all the believers" addressed by Paul in his first letter to the Church in Thessalonica: "The word of the Lord has echoed forth from you resoundingly . . . throughout every region your faith in God is celebrated, which makes it needless for us to say anything more" (1 Thess 1:8, NAB).

***TIME OUT!

You are invited to think about what you have been reading. Please consider these questions, either on your own or in discussion with others.

1. As a catechist, who or what motivates you? What is your understanding of your catechetical role in your school or parish catechetical program?

2. What have you had to give up in order to engage in catechetical ministry in your school or parish? What have you gained from this ministry?

3. When you are preparing a catechetical session for the children you teach, what part requires most of your planning time and attention?

1

Discovering Lectionary-Based Catechesis

Liturgy Then and Now

When I was a child growing up in the pre-Vatican II church, attending Mass was a mystical but quite puzzling experience for me. Much of what was happening was far beyond my powers of understanding. The bows, mumblings, and genuflections spoke to me of inscrutable rituals enacted for unknown reasons. The most prominent feature at the altar was the priest's back, and the words that issued from his mouth were incomprehensible and therefore assumed a magical significance. It was all wonderfully mysterious and filled me with awe.

However, I eventually began to truly welcome and appreciate that part of the Mass that came after all the bending and breast-beating and strange Latin phrases ("*Mea culpa, mea culpa, mea maxima culpa . . .*"), when the priest at last turned to face us and began to speak and read in words I could finally understand. To be sure, most of the actual significance of those words eluded me, but to hear the epistle and the gospel read in a language I recognized was a great joy (and relief!) to me after all that mumbling in Latin. As I remember it, the *experience* of hearing those words and stories made a far greater impact on me than the vague comprehension of the actual meaning of the words. And yet the stories were vivid, told in a vigorous voice by a dramatic reader attired in exotic and colorful robes, and often resounding from within a cloud of incense.

As a child of the pre-TV era, I appreciated the entertainment value of Mass. This was as close to live action theater as I ever got. At the children's Mass every Sunday morning at 9:00 we were required to sit with our peers, in the front of the church, and I loved being so close to the action. I felt sorry for my parents who had to sit in the back and couldn't see or hear or smell all this excitement. I admired the boys who got to serve on the altar, ringing bells and holding golden plates under the chins of communicants. Since I couldn't do that, I watched a lot, tried to connect the Latin on the left side of the missal with the English on the right side, and rose and sat and stood and knelt with great gusto throughout the whole event. I really had little idea what was going on, but I entered enthusiastically into the experience of collective blissful ignorance.

Today's children don't have to struggle with the Tridentine Mass and its mysterious language and ritual. Today's children have, instead, the opportunity to participate in a communal celebration that they can understand. While I remember enjoying the experience of Mass, I certainly did not understand it or in any way see that what was going on there had any connection whatsoever to the rest of my life. Sunday mornings were an isolated part of my week, and not until much much later in my mature wisdom did I begin to grasp how I might take something of that experience away with me for further reflection, thought, or response. For me as a child, the gospel readings were stories about long ago, and what Jesus said or did had nothing to do with me. Many children today might well be experiencing the same distancing from liturgical symbol and ritual, especially when those rituals and symbols are poorly expressed. But there's a much better chance that today's liturgy will allow children to see, hear, smell, taste, and feel the community's worship experience and to know that they are a part of that experience.

While many agree that contemporary liturgical experience lacks certain elements of the drama and sense of transcendence found in the past, there is probably little argument that the silence, words, gestures, smells, food and drink, movements, music, images and prayers of today's Eucharistic Liturgy are vibrant symbols that present a strong and clear expression of the essentials of thanksgiving, offering and response that are constitutive of our most profound form of public worship. But it hasn't always been this way.

I count myself as one of the fortunate generation who can well remember Mass BVT (Before Vatican Two). Young people today view us as quaint relics of a bygone era who sit on their BVT rocking-chairs telling endless tales of "growing up Catholic" with a combination of nostalgia and dismay. But I, and many of my friends, truly enjoy looking at Church Past without any sense of Dickensian humbug and remember with fondness the people, places, and events of those days that certainly helped to shape my current attitudes about God and Church.

It is true that some of these memories reveal "quaint" liturgical practices. My male friends who were once altar boys remember watching and listening carefully for the priest to signal that the bells should be rung, and remember with shame the times they misinterpreted the signals and jingled away at the wrong time. The boys were able to observe things that I, a girl trapped in the pew, could not see because the priest bowing and facing the altar with his back to me obscured the view: the tight and controlled gestures that never went outside the orbit of his body, his thumb and index figures held tightly together after the consecration, the many little crosses and kissings of holy and sacred things.

I remember observing only the priest's back encased in fiddle-shaped chasuble, and still have vague images of billowing lace-edged surplices worn by the priests who distributed communion to us at the communion rail, proceeding from left to right ("from Mary to Joseph") and then circling and swirling around again back to the left side. I also remember the so-called "last gospel" and the prayers for the conversion of Russia, which ran together and which I always seemed to get confused. It was not until I encountered the "beginning of the holy gospel according to St. John" in the actual Bible that I realized that this passage did not include some Hail Mary's and the words "Hail, Holy Queen, Mother of Mercy, our life, our sweetness, and our hope . . ."

The liturgical reforms of Vatican II turned the altar and the priest around, in more ways than one. Now we could all watch, observe, and—yes—criticize what was going on in front of us. Priests who had learned to "say" Mass in Latin, and who could get away with mumbled and mysterious incantations that they suspected had little meaning for the faithful, all at once needed to not only learn a whole new series of prayers *in English* but to expreess these prayers clearly so that all could hear and respond. Even those of us out there in the pews could now see and observe and watch and hear what was happening at the altar.

It seemed that each week there was something new. The altar rails disappeared one day. We began to sing. Guitars appeared, played by nuns in real clothes who led the music from—of all things—the front of the church. Statues fell and banners took their place. Certainly the recitation of prayers in the vernacular was the most striking innovation next to the experience of actually seeing the priest's face throughout the whole Mass. There seemed to be a lot of confusion and misinterpretation of meanings and symbols as there often is during a period of transition from old to new.

As liturgical reforms buffeted us from every direction, we all became instant experts in liturgy. Our "expertise" arose out of nothing more than a personal preference for a certain style or way of worshiping. My father, a classical musician in his youth, could not stand the guitars and purposefully stayed away from Masses where they were played. My children, on the other hand, loved the guitar music and sang along lustily. Liturgy committees became the rage in parishes, and the presence of these unprofessional critics of liturgical style pressured the poor presiders to update their communication skills and to learn how to present a dramatic performance Sunday after Sunday.

Some of this was certainly healthy and good, but a lot of it was probably an unnecessary but normal response to change. Some of the confusion could have been avoided by effective catechetical preparation for the changes that were "imposed" by Vatican decree. When the new Rites of Penance were promulgated in the mid-1970's, my diocese presented a series of instructional gatherings in parishes to explain the rationale and to catechize us about what to expect and why. As a result there seemed to be little resistance or confusion, and people in my parish not only accepted the new rites but even began very soon to use "reconciliation" rather than "going to confession" language. Other liturgical reforms might have been less problematic had this approach been used more consistently.

Eventually, however, things began to settle down and most people accommodated to the new ways of doing things at Mass. Today, liturgical expression is a mixture of the old and the new, coming out of a dynamic that refuses to be contained in only one form of expression.

Further along in this book we will explore ways in which lectionary-based catechesis has evolved out of the past and into the present world of catechetics. In doing this we can come to a renewed appreciation for the turmoil that has finally resulted in not only acceptance of the role of liturgy in our catechetical endeavors but also great enthusiasm for the potential that lectionary-based catechesis presents to us.

The Liturgy of the Word Then and Now

The liturgical reforms of Vatican II had a particular impact on the Liturgy of the Word as these reforms not only brought English into our churches but presented us with additional scripture stories from both Christian and Hebrew scripture and asked for homilies that would make connections between the Word proclaimed and the life experiences of the faithful. With the growing accent on the equal importance of the Liturgy of the Word and the Liturgy of the Eucharist, people gradually began to value the contribution scripture could make to the total liturgical celebration. Many of us were taught that in order to fulfill the Sunday Mass obligation you must arrive in time to hear the reading of the gospel and you cannot leave until after communion. This certainly lost a lot of its meaning when we were exposed to well-proclaimed readings and a rich appreciation for the entire liturgical celebration.

Eventually, in 1969, the Sacred Congregation for Divine Worship published the three-year cycle lectionary of readings featuring a different synoptic gospel each year, with the fourth gospel scattered throughout all three cycles but receiving special emphasis during the Lenten and Easter seasons. Many defects have been noted and criticisms aimed at the way the lectionary was designed: the often incomprehensible connection (or even lack of connection) between Old Testament and New Testament readings, the long summer "bread" discourses from the sixth chapter of John in Cycle B that present such a challenge to homilists to keep finding something new to say each week about bread and eucharist, the selective editing of the psalms to present an overly generous and triumphant God, and of course the lack of inclusive language present in the current translation.

For all of its deficiencies, however, this lectionary was revolutionary: it presents a much greater selection and variety of scripture over a period of three years, not one. The first reading, from Hebrew scripture, while not always connected in clear ways to the gospel, at least presents a much broader and more complete picture of the unfolding of salvation history among the Israelite community. For homilists, this picture presents bright and vivid images that enhance understanding and interpretation of the gospels. If the homilist is really astute, creative, and knows something about exegesis and biblical criticism, the homilist can at times even see connections within the second reading as well which provide a framework that sets off the entire Liturgy of the Word.

The lectionary as we know it today is a relatively new liturgical experience for Catholics, and yet how quickly we have become accustomed to its face. Sometimes for nostalgia's sake I take out my old St. Joseph's Missal and make comparisons, and I must say the missal readings seem terribly meager and limited. In the middle of Lent there is no Samaritan woman at the well to remind us of our baptismal call to overcome sin and tell others of the new life of Jesus' love. On the final Sunday of Advent there was no opportunity for those of us who are mothers to relate to Mary's impending motherhood and to contemplate God's presence through the mysteries of conception, pregnancy, and birth. During the "green season" of Sundays "after Pentecost" (when the priest always wore green vestments) there was a great deal of jumping around from gospel to gospel with no apparent order: in one series the missal proceeds from Luke 17 ("Saving Faith") to Matthew 6 ("Confidence in the Lord of Life") to Luke 7 ("The Dead Live") to Luke 14 ("God Spurns the Proud") and so on.

The lectionary today, although far from perfect, does much better with continuity, diversity, and relevance to the liturgical season. The cycle of lectionary readings not only offers a close look at each gospel in turn but also provides the script as the stage is set for a deeper appreciation of each liturgical season. The Liturgy of the Word is the medium through which we as Catholic Christians tell and listen to our stories and remember our faith tradition. The setting where this takes place contributes greatly to an authentic experience of worship and prayer. In parishes where attention is given to creative and cohesive liturgical expression the environment of the worship space indeed describes in living color and texture just where we are at any given season of the year. Homilies are truly homiletic in that they nudge a faith response from the hearers of the Word. The assembly has learned to expect music selections that enhance and reflect the readings of the day while encouraging even the non-musical to sing their hearts out. All of this contributes to our life of faith and also to our ability to express our faith.

***TIME OUT!

Again you are invited to reflect upon what you have been reading. Please think about these questions, either on your own or in discussion with others.

1. What do I remember about "going to church" when I was a child? Who, if anyone, went with me? How did I get there? What made the greatest impression on me? Why?

2. What makes the greatest impression on me when I "go to church" today?

3. If I could change one thing about liturgy at my parish, it would be to_____.

Liturgical Catechesis

To appreciate the value of lectionary-based catechesis, then, it is important to begin with some clarifications of the relationship between liturgy and catechesis. The concept of liturgical catechesis needs to be defined and developed if lectionary-based catechesis is to be understood.

When we take a brief look at the ways in which liturgy has developed throughout the past years since Vatican II, we recognize anew the important relationship between good liturgical expression and good catechetical expression. Both liturgy and catechesis have in common a major but quite basic purpose: to lead people to God. This is not to say that the two paths leading to God are alike, or even parallel, but certainly they converge at certain points and reach the same destination.

Both catechists and liturgists agree that "liturgy is not catechesis is not liturgy," and yet in many ways the two are existentially intertwined. We can say the experience of good liturgy catechizes if we propose the broad definition of "catechesis" the way it is used in #21 in the *General Catechetical Directory* (Sacred Congregation for the Clergy, United States Catholic Conference: Washington, D.C., 1971): "that form of ecclesial action which leads both communities and individual members of the faithful to maturity of faith." We can also say that the experience of good liturgy is enhanced by catechesis before, during, and after the experience: spiritual preparation and pondering the meaning of the Word to be proclaimed beforehand (a DRE I know calls it "getting in the mood for Mass"), active and conscious participation in the actual liturgical celebration while it is going on, and setting aside some personal reflection time in church before leaving, on the way home, or whenever there might be a peaceful moment later.

Andrew Varga describes this process of what he calls "Spiritual Preparation, Celebration, and Reflection-Mission" in his excellent article "The Three Moments of Liturgical Catechesis" in the March, 1993 issue of *Catechumenate: A Journal of Christian Initiation.* He makes the distinction between catechesis as didactic methodology and catechesis as an evocative-reflective experience. Didactic methodology is in no way appropriate for the liturgical celebration, but when reflection on the liturgical experience evokes a deeper faith response, catechesis is recognized as having an authentic and complementary partnership with liturgy.

Of course we must let liturgy be liturgy—an experience of public prayer and worship in the midst of one's community of faith—and not expect to teach or to be taught in a formal way while there. The maxim is "Relax and enjoy!" and yet we can also expect to be changed, or even to be transformed. If we leave the eucharistic assembly more willing to serve and care for others, more capable of tolerance and forgiveness, more persuaded that injustice can be overcome and more aware that we can be a part of doing that, and more convinced that because of God's love we can begin to change our own nasty—and yes, even sinful—ways, then somehow we have learned something about God, Church, Jesus, sacraments, morality, and our faith tradition.

The questions posed in the earlier section of this chapter can prod us to do some clear thinking about just what the liturgical experience means to us in our lives today. I was amused during the weekend of the

Blizzard of 1993 when I heard that because of the record snowfall in the eastern part of the United States and consequent concern for safety of travelers, the archbishop of Baltimore had dispensed his faithful from the obligation to attend Mass on that Sunday. I lived at the time in Cleveland where there is a vast supply of snowplows and road salt, and so we were not dispensed from the "obligation": indeed, although the storm was quite violent and nearly every other religious denomination cancelled services it was taken for granted that Catholics in Cleveland would tough it out and would be there for Mass. There seems to be something in our tradition as Catholics that has led us to the mentality of getting to Mass "no matter what" unless we're told we don't have to, and I wonder at times how much it has to do with a deep hunger for worship. But stressing the importance of coming together as a community of faith to pray is of course a worthy and commendable activity, if we can go beyond the "obligation" part. On that snowy and frigid Sunday I thought about how we might respond to a dispensation from the obligation to attend Mass if it were given on a warm and balmy June day. How many of us would stay away? How many would come anyway, because of a sincere desire to be there? What choice would I make?

For most of us, liturgy is the ritualized expression of the faith of the religious community to which we have a sense of belonging and obligation. This implies that we are participants in a ritual that has significance for us, that expresses the values and beliefs that we have come to acknowledge as our own. If we take this concept seriously, it means we take the ritual with us when we leave church and make it part of our daily lives. We can do this in many ways, of course, one of which involves real participation in the Word of God as it shapes and gives purpose to our mission of loving service to others.

Having said that, we need to go further. In doing liturgy as well as in doing lectionary-based catechesis it is as important to know what not to do as to know what to do. The duel that continues between liturgists and catechists exemplifies the dichotomy that exists in attempting to express the experience of God in two different ways. And yet many insist that there are more similarities than differences between liturgy and catechesis as expressions of God's presence among us.

The success of any catechetical experience depends greatly on the quality of liturgy that forms and transforms the worshiping community. The success of liturgy depends greatly on the quality of catechesis that expresses the faith of the catechetical community. Once a few basic definitions are in place and are agreed upon and after some misconceptions are erased it seems possible to agree that the two occupy a shared dependency on each other. Liturgists and catechists have established a long-term, albeit uneasy marriage, knowing in their souls that "we can't get along with them and we can't get along without them."

The generic definition of "liturgy" has been traditionally understood as the "work" of the people or, as defined by Fr. Richard McBrien, "the official public worship of the church, especially eucharist and the sacraments." This seems simple enough to all who are not "professional" liturgists. Professional liturgists may expand that definition to include many nuanced expressions of "public worship" that are all tied up with rubrics, rites, and ritual actions. However, if one were to ask a typical fifth grade Catholic child, as I did once, we might expect her to answer that "Liturgy is what we do on Sunday mornings at church." I think for our purposes here that that's a pretty fair definition.

"Catechesis" has many official definitions gleaned from many official church documents such as the one mentioned earlier from the 1971 General Catechetical Directory that "catechesis" is the term to be used "for that form of ecclesial action which leads both communities and individual members of the faithful to maturity of faith." A slightly more nuanced way of stating the same thing is found in Paragraph 75 of the *Rite of Christian Initiation of Adults* which speaks of catechesis that is appropriate for catechumens: the "suitable pastoral formation and guidance, aimed at training them in the Christian life." In both cases, catechesis is understood to be much much more than indoctrination, instruction, or memorization.

At a consultation at Belleville, Illinois, in November, 1991 sponsored by The North American Forum on the Catechumenate, catechists and liturgists came together to begin discussions on the nature of the two disciplines and to find ways to arrive at a common definition for "liturgical catechesis." It was agreed early in the conference that definitions were the first order of the day before fruitful dialogue could take place. After a good deal of discreet turf-guarding and polite disagreements, the two groups managed to begin to dialogue and even to concur on many points of similarity. Liturgical catechesis, it appears, brings together the best of liturgy and the best of catechesis and results in an enhanced faith experience. I'm not sure a three-day consultation process is required to arrive at that conclusion.

Once upon a time when I was young and untrained in catechetical theory, I "just knew" that the Mass was somehow instrumental in teaching me something about God. There was even a time when I identified within the Mass the exact moments when I was sure God was being made real for me by the priest: during the scripture readings, when I received the host in holy communion, and when we, the congregation, sang together. At that time, when I was still young and untrained, the

Second Vatican Council had not yet proclaimed the wonderful notion in *The Constitution on the Sacred Liturgy,* #7, that Jesus is equally present in the Eucharistic Liturgy in the presider, in the Word, in the sacrament of the eucharist, and in the assembly. But intuitively I knew I was indeed learning something about Jesus and God and Church, just by being there Sunday after Sunday and paying attention.

I think, today, that liturgical catechesis is something like that. We come, week after week, and join with friends and family to somehow celebrate the reality of God with us. We are assembled and guided, we listen, we share the eucharistic bread and wine, we join with one another in prayer, and God is there in our midst. This is catechesis at its best, liturgy at its best.

At the Belleville consultation, liturgy and catechesis came together most profoundly in the "work of the people" that took place at a liturgical celebration in memory of Christiane Brusselmans, the Belgian catechist who had died a few weeks earlier. Christiane had been instrumental in designing a highly regarded program for the sacramental preparation of children and was a driving force behind the process for implementing Christian initiation of adults and children when the *Rite of Christian Initiation of Adults* was promulgated in 1972.

Many at that consultation had known and loved Christiane deeply, and all had been greatly inspired by her contributions to the worlds of both catechesis and sacramental celebration. The liturgy in Belleville was a re-creation of her funeral Mass in Belgium, with much of the same music, readings, and even a repeat of the eulogy/homily given by Fr. Jim Dunning. The entire liturgical experience was indeed "work" of the people, a grieving process that engaged us all in the common effort of mourning.

For me, the entire liturgical experience was also catechetical, in that it brought me closer to the "maturity of faith" that I often seek in other settings. This was indeed an "ecclesial action" as it was connected to the life of the people of God, the Church. The liturgical experience was certainly not intended to "teach" us anything, but rather was a celebration of the life and death of someone well-loved by all who were there.

I was not acquainted with Christiane Brusselmans personally, although I had encountered her many times at workshops and had heard her speak on numerous occasions over the years. But in that liturgical experience I came to truly know her. I learned about Christiane's sense of humor, her dedication to catechesis and to the process of initiation, her persistence, her closeness to her family, her special love for children.

I also learned, as if for the first time, about resurrection that emerges out of death and mourning, about the new life of loving service that is possible when we "die to ourselves," about a God who mourns with us but who also transforms us in our letting go. The readings taught me, the homily/eulogy taught me, the music taught me, the experience of hundreds of friends all sharing Christiane stories and tears and eucharist taught me. This was indeed liturgical catechesis. To come to such a level of understanding of the mystery of death, of new life, and of the impact of one person's faith, neither component—liturgy or catechesis—could have been omitted.

However, there is always that other dimension of "knowing," and it cannot be ignored. Catechists, who lead people to maturity of faith, must indeed also find ways to lead people to a more profound knowledge of the faith tradition. The relationship of catechesis and liturgy is a complicated one, but when it comes down to the catechetical basics we might say, as Rita Ferrone and Fr. Bob Duggan stated at the Belleville consultation, that "catechesis can prepare people for liturgy and motivate people to return to liturgy." In order that this be accomplished, however, a methodology and a consistent and intentional system needs to be in place. This implies some kind of formal catechesis, to adapt Andrew Varga's notion, both before and after liturgy.

While liturgy is happening, everyone now seems to agree, is definitely not the time to do any catechesis of a formal nature. However, I didn't always possess the wisdom I have acquired through many years of catechetical experience. At one period in my catechetical development I allowed a quite awful so-called learning experience to take place. I arranged a "grade level" Mass for the fifth grade children in our parish religious education program. I requested that Father use this occasion to teach the children all about the Mass by demonstrating as he went along. He, being just as catechetically under-developed as I was, did what I asked. He stopped and explained the meaning and significance of every gesture, every piece of liturgical apparatus, every shift from one action to the next. The children were bored silly, and were embarrassingly normal in their squirming and not-so-quiet whispers. The whole thing dragged on and on in a most tedious way and never seemed to engage anyone in either worship or catechesis.

I learned a lot from that experience, and that priest did too. We agreed that to allow liturgy to catechize we must allow the children to experience a liturgy that was indeed a communal celebration, not a communal demonstration. We would, in the future, prepare them for liturgy with some hands-on activities in the back-stage area, seeing close up what liturgical vestments and vessels are like. We would—ahead of time—explain simply and without lengthy detail the dramatic flow of the Mass, from gathering to contrition to listening to stories to responding to offering to eating to thanking and finally to going forth.

We were not yet quite far enough along in our understanding of the difference between liturgy and catechesis to make that final leap, to allow some real catechetical time *after* the liturgical experience for the children to reflect on what happened and to respond further in faith. Now I know better, and I hope that priest of long ago does also. It would be nice to look him up someday and reminisce with him about our mutual blunders and to compare notes about what we learned from them. I pray for those children whose faith might have stumbled as we stumbled, but with humility I must acknowledge that the experience more than likely left little impact on them one way or the other. As always, in every catechetical endeavor, we cannot underestimate the importance of trusting in God's grace.

In preparing children (or adults, for that matter) for liturgy by means of some kind of formal catechesis beforehand and in allowing reflection to occur following the celebration, we in no way want to indicate that a "rehearsal" mentality be in place. Of course participation in liturgy as presiders, greeters, altar servers, readers, eucharistic ministers, or homilists demands a fair amount of prayerful preparation. Those engaged in specific liturgical ministry expect to plan ahead. But for others, the assembly in general, a simple and general understanding of what to expect and why is important.

For many, this occurs naturally over the course of some years, as it happened to me in my childhood. For others, there may be a need to bring to a conscious level the meaning of the words, actions, and rituals that they are experiencing at Mass. This demythologizing of the liturgical mystery can have an adverse effect, however, if children (or any of us who become very familiar with the ritual) regard the liturgical experience as a predictable and/or predetermined script complete with the same props, stagehands, and theatrical directions. The changing and evolving liturgical seasons along with constant awareness of how God's word continues to speak to us as our lives unfold bring to the liturgical experience a sense of ever-newness and even surprise. That is why we allow the experience to speak for itself, to wash over us and engulf us with new insight into what God is like.

While liturgy is happening, we involve ourselves in the experience, praying our way through the ritual and allowing God to be present to us in word, sacrament, presider, and each other. We do not strain to understand or to interpret the experience while it is going on: we simply, as those cute young waiters at jazzy restaurants always tell us when they bring our food, "Enjoy!"

So we are starting to see that lectionary-based catechesis begins when liturgy and catechesis come together in a particular and specific way. Catechesis often "just happens" within the liturgical experience. Lectionary readings play an important part in formal catechetical sessions. Liturgy and catechesis are both vital in the faith life of children, and lectionary-based catechesis can be an important way to link the liturgical experience with the catechetical experience. More about all of this in the next section.

***TIME OUT!

Once again you are invited to reflect upon what you have been reading. Please consider the following questions, either on your own or in discussion with others.

1. Define in your own words the meaning of "liturgical catechesis."

2. Think of a liturgical experience that brought you new insight or understanding concerning your relationship with God, church, or others. What was there about that liturgy that affected you in that way?

3. Why is liturgy sometimes defined as "work of the people"?

Some resources that might be helpful for further insight and understanding:

John Paul II. *Catechesi Tradendae (On Catechesis in Our Time)*. Boston: Daughters of St. Paul, 1979.

McBrien, Richard. *Catholicism*. Minneapolis: Winston Press, 1981.

United States Catholic Bishops. *Sharing the Light of Faith: The National Catechetical Directory for Catholics in the United States*. Washington, D.C.: United States Catholic Conference, 1979.

Varga, Andrew. "The Three Moments of Liturgical Catechesis," *Catechumenate: A Journal of Christian Initiation,* Volume 15, No. 2 (March, 1993), pp. 13–21.

2

The Development of
Lectionary-Based Catechesis

Liturgy and Catechesis

In the last chapter liturgy and catechesis are presented as distinct but equal partners, both of which are necessary for the birth, growth and development of lectionary-based catechesis. Separating the two would be fatal. Together, they become greater than the sum of their parts. The symbiosis that exists between liturgy and catechesis can be appropriated by both catechists and liturgists to bring about the transformation and conversion that can be the results, the offspring, of this union.

But what is an effective way to nurture and encourage this mutual alliance? How do we bring to birth the unity of purpose both liturgy and catechesis possess? One key element that can aid in the delivery of healthy progeny is good pre-natal care: access to healthful food and exercise, regular contact with the ones who are to assist with the birthing process, truth in the goodness of the natural process of procreation, and enthusiasm for the project of bringing new life into the world. Lectionary-based catechesis can come to birth out of the healthy and productive union of liturgy and catechesis.

One way that liturgy and catechesis come together to bring new life into the world of the worshiping community is through the lectionary readings which are the natural issue of this fruitful union. Good pre-natal care is important if the lectionary is to come to life in fulfillment of its purpose. An understanding of the meaning and significance of the scriptures brings the nourishment that is necessary for developing faith to thrive and grow. The process of procreation of faith is a natural outcome when those responsible for assisting in this endeavor are enthusiastic, trusting, and convinced of the goodness of the emerging new life.

It is certainly in the best interest of the child that both parents contribute to the child's welfare, as any parent who has had to do it all alone will agree. So it is in lectionary-based catechesis which reflects the parentage of both catechesis and liturgy. When both parents are responsible for the continuing sustenance of their offspring, healthy and productive growth is most likely to occur. Both parents—liturgy and catechesis—need to be consistently and effectively present if lectionary-based catechesis is to grow and flourish.

Paul writes of the interaction between both parents—liturgy and cate-chesis—in his wonderful description of an early eucharistic celebration in 1 Cor. 11:23 ff: "I received from the Lord what I handed on to you, namely, that the Lord Jesus, on the night in which he was betrayed, took bread. . . . Every time, then, you eat this bread and drink this cup, you proclaim the death of the Lord until he comes!" When Paul "handed on to you" what was received "from the Lord," he is catechist/parent. When Paul insists that "every time" we eat and drink in this manner we "proclaim" our faith, he is liturgist/parent. In the contemporary liturgical scene, this passage is read at the start of the Easter Triduum on Holy Thursday and again on the Feast of Corpus Christi in Cycle C. We also come across it in liturgies commemorating the eucharist and even on an obscure Monday in the 24th week of the year. And each time we hear what "has been handed on" to us, we encounter those parents of ours—catechesis *and* liturgy—who gave us a life centered on God's Word that is most clearly understood in the lived proclamation of eating and drinking together "until he comes!"

Liturgical celebrations from the earliest Christian times contained elements of catechesis along with prayer and the reading of scripture, as described in Acts 2:42: "They devoted themselves to the apostles' in-struction and the communal life, to the breaking of bread and the prayers." As Fr. Raymond Brown states in *The New Jerome Biblical Commentary,* 80 (13): "Authoritative for all Jews were the Scriptures, in particular the Law and the Prophets; this would have been true for the first followers of Jesus as well. Thus, early Christian teaching would for the most part have been Jewish teaching. . . . Points where Jesus modi-fied or differed . . . were remembered and became the nucleus of a special teaching. . . . when such teaching was eventually committed to writing, those writings had within themselves the possibility of becoming a second set of sacred Scriptures (the NT)."

So the coming together of liturgy and catechesis in what we have come to call "liturgical catechesis" is not all that new. However, the current turmoil among catechists and liturgists concerning this matter would indicate the contrary. The development of religious education theory in the United States throughout the twentieth century, as we will see in the next section, has tended toward the separation of liturgy and catechesis. Liturgists, who have often viewed catechesis as a didactic, instructional excercise, have not always recognized ways in which catechesis can be a viable part of the liturgical experience. As a result, lectionary-based catechesis is sometimes seen as a "neither-nor" anomaly rather than the means to bring together both liturgy and catechesis. In spite of persuasive analogies and in spite of certain aspects of early Christian tradition, it can be difficult to see how liturgy and catechesis can fit together. Perhaps this can become more clear if we take a closer look at the development of lectionary-based catechesis as it has evolved within the process of Christian initiation.

Catechesis and the Order of Christian Initiation

Just where did this idea of using the lectionary as the basis for catechesis come from? Why did someone have to muddy the calm curriculum-based catechetical waters with this unpredictable upstart? It seemed much simpler when as catechists our greatest challenge was to understand and use Shared Christian Praxis. Now we not only use good catechetical methodology, as Shared Christian Praxis certainly is, but we have found ways to incorporate that methodology into a catechetical process that builds on the process of initiation that has been with us since earliest times. And so, to understand lectionary-based catechesis we must begin with an understanding of Christian initiation.

In the early church, small communities of Christians brought new members into their midst by introducing them gradually into the new way of life taught and lived by Jesus. Eventually, by around the third or fourth century, the catechumenate as we know it today took on a more formal shape that included catechesis, certain requirements for initiation, and liturgical celebration of the rites of initiation in stages. Today, the restoration of the catechumenate has led to a restoration of catechesis that goes back to the ancient roots of earliest Christianity.

There has been a gradual development in the catechesis of adults preparing for initiation since the Second Vatican Council "prescribed the revision of the rite of baptism of adults and decreed that the catechumenate for adults in several stages be restored," as stated in the 1972 Decree by the Congregation for Divine Worship. The *Rite of Christian Initiation of Adults* was eventually translated into English and in September, 1988, was mandated by the American bishops for use in all dioceses of the United States. This process to be used in the Christian initiation of adults has been adopted as the norm for bringing adults to the sacraments of baptism, confirmation, and eucharist.

The rites of initiation indicate plainly just how this is to be done: in stages according to evidence of conversion and of the candidate's readiness and desire for initiation. The catechetical and liturgical processes during the time of preparation for initiation are clearly based on and contained within the community's liturgical experience. Because of the ancient traditions surrounding the restored catechumenate, the liturgical year itself forms the context for initiation: Easter and baptism are inseparable. It was inevitable that the lectionary, reflecting the seasons and stages of the liturgical year, would become an essential catechetical as well as liturgical component in leading candidates and catechumens through the seasons and stages of conversion in preparation for initiation.

Before the restoration of the catechumenate, a typical catechetical session for those wanting to "become Catholics" followed the *Fr. Smith Instructs Jackson* approach. This popular book (by Bishop John F. Noll, published by Our Sunday Visitor Press, Huntington, Indiana in 1950) portrayed "convert class" sessions which consisted of ongoing conversations between a priest and a layman who was interested in Catholicism. In these fictionalized sessions, the layman had all the questions (brief and to the point) and the priest had all the answers (lengthy and extremely detailed) concerning God, church, morality, salvation, and every kind of Catholic practice and tradition. Becoming a Catholic, of course, was the ultimate goal of these sessions.

In preparing people for initiation today through the order of Christian initiation of adults, catechesis takes quite a different tack. Catechumens are gently confronted with issues of prayer, formation, conversion, and apostolic endeavors as they encounter and ponder the Liturgy of the Word week by week by week. The lectionary plays a vital part in their "pastoral formation" as the Word evolves out of the liturgical year and is proclaimed within the community of believers.

The catechesis of adult catechumens takes place following the liturgical celebration of the Word and allows sacred scripture to speak, inform, and transform. Following the Rite of Acceptance into the Order of Catechumens and during the entire period of the catechumenate, catechumens and their catechist are blessed by the presider and are "sent forth" from Mass following the homily. They go to a place prepared for them to reflect on the Word they have just experienced and to discover and discern within the scriptures some insight into the nature of God, Church, and their own spirituality. The content of catechesis, guided carefully and with sensitivity by the catechist, emerges from the questions and discussions surrounding the lectionary readings and the homiletic reflections.

Ideally, the catechetical session continues long enough to allow adequate time for group discussion, sponsor-catechumen sharing, and prayer response. This means, of course, that the catechetical session extends beyond the end of the parish liturgy. Many parishes encourage sponsors, family members, candidates for full communion, the rest of the catechetical team, and hospitality persons to join the catechumens for these Sunday sessions.

In other parishes the scripture session ends with the conclusion of Mass, and the catechetical session is continued on a weekday evening— but always with another proclamation of the lectionary readings, prayer response, and brief homiletic reminder. In both cases, the scripture readings found in the lectionary, while limited in scope, provide the basis out of which can emerge some content for catechesis, a format for prayer, and opportunities for response.

Lectionary-based catechesis, then, developed out of this "back to the future" retrieval of the catechumenal process of the ancient church. It was rediscovered that adults didn't really need to know all they never wanted to know about Catholicism in a few short weeks in order to be prepared for the sacraments of initiation. Rather, in the restored catechumenate there is emphasis on conversion along with knowledge as criteria for initiation. This means that the "suitable catechesis . . . planned to be gradual and complete in its coverage, accommodated to the liturgical year, and solidly supported by celebrations of the word" described in #75.1 of the *Rite of Christian Initiation of Adults,* begins with weekly encounters with the Word within the community liturgical celebration. Lectionary-based catechesis, building on the liturgical celebration, offers opportunities to investigate content with the ultimate intention of conversion to mission and service.

***TIME OUT!

Again you are invited to reflect upoon what you have been reading. Please consider these questions, either on your own or in discussion with others:

1. How do the lectionary readings catechize?

2. Do you see any similarities between liturgical or lectionary-based catechesis and a session with "Fr. Smith"? If so, what are they? If not, why not?

3. Do you have any questions about Catholicism that you've always wanted to ask?

Initiation of Children of a Catechetical Age

It wasn't long before the concepts of catechesis for adult catechumens began to invade catechesis for unbaptized children who were old enough to understand and participate in their own initiation. The process of preparing children of a catechetical age for the sacraments of baptism, confirmation, and eucharist, according to Part II of the order of Christian initiation, follows the adult model. This means respecting and implementing the same stages of initiation that adults experience: the pre-catechumenate time of inquiry, the catechumenate time of discovery and learning, the time of enlightenment and immediate prayerful preparation for the Easter sacraments, and the time of mystagogy which begins a life-long investigation into the meaning of God's love.

Lectionary-based catechesis offers to both adults and children the week by week by week experience of the Word, out of which emerges whatever doctrinal content is actually present in those scripture passages. As with the adults, liturgical celebrations mark the stages of initiation as the children proceed along their own unique spiritual journeys.

Signs of conversion and readiness for the rites of initiation leading to baptism, confirmation, and eucharist are evidenced in many ways. Minimal cognitive knowledge is necessary for the reception of the sacraments of initiation. Indeed, Catholic teaching clearly indicates from the time of Pius X's 1910 encyclical on the eucharist, *Quam Singulari,* that children need only a simple understanding of the nature of the bread and wine consumed at eucharist. The current *Code of Canon Law* states this equally clearly in #913: to come to eucharist, children must be prepared so that they can "understand the mystery of Christ according to their capacity, and can receive the Body of the Lord with faith and devotion."

Preparation for baptism and confirmation is just as simple: confirmation is the completion of baptism, a transitional sacrament that Linda Gaupin insists "seals what was begun in baptism and leads to eucharist, the fullness and completion of the initiatory process" (from "Now Confirmation Needs Its Own *Quam Singulari,*" in *When Should We Confirm,* James A. Wilde, ed., Chicago: Liturgy Training Publications, 1989, p. 91). It seems therefore that whatever is taught about baptism can be taught regarding confirmation: that children need to know and experience something about the faith community into which they will be initiated. The practices, celebrations, and lived faith of the community so influence the children that their eagerness and desire to participate and be a part of it is an important indicator of readiness for initiation.

The ability of the children to pray and to worship and their willingness and intention to learn more about what the faith community believes and stands for are also signs of readiness for initiation. The children celebrate the stages of readiness through the rite of entrance into the catechumenate, the rite of election (optional for children), the adapted scrutiny rites, and, in time, they may be baptized, confirmed, and receive eucharist at the Easter Vigil along with the adults or at some time during the Easter season.

Lectionary-based catechesis, then, has been used in this very basic form in the process of preparing both adults and children of a catechetical age for the sacraments of initiation. This appears to be a natural by-product of the process of catechesis for initiation that connects to liturgical seasons and celebrations, always within the context of the community of faith. Fr. Smith no longer instructs Mr. Jackson in didactic lectures. Now, Fr. Smith may well be part of a catechumenate team that gently assists those preparing for initiation to "break open" the Word and to discover there the living God who speaks of conversion and loving service.

As parish communities became more and more comfortable with the order of Christian initiation of adults (and of children of a catechetical age) it wasn't long before the catechetical community began to catch on. Lectionary-based catechesis for children was bound to happen. When religious educators and catechetical leaders—and ordinary catechists as well—began to observe how lectionary-based catechesis was being experienced by adults and children preparing for initiation, lights began to flash and bells began to ring. There was a sense that this "method" was real, authentic, and had possibilities for use with ordinary, already-baptized children as well.

Once it became evident that there was a place for the concept of liturgical catechesis within the framework of our common experience as eucharistic people, it was possible go on to consider some specific ways in which this concept could be integrated into formal, systematic, intentional catechetical programs.

Lectionary-based catechesis can be a continuation of the process of growth that begins with Sunday liturgy. Very simply put, lectionary-based catechesis can also be experienced in a formal, intentional, and systematic process that looks to the Sunday lectionary readings for its content and methodology. Like much in our faith tradition, lectionary-based catechesis is much easier to define than to put into practice. But like the liturgical reforms mentioned earlier, lectionary-based catechesis evolved out of an awareness of human needs, and some creative yet logical ways to meet these needs have been gradually developed.

As catechists, we might certainly want to question what effect these liturgical reforms have had on the process of traditional catechesis in our child-centered programs. And as catechists, we might certainly realize that until quite recently there has been very little notice taken of the role of the Sunday lectionary readings in considering curriculum design, content, or methodology. Instead, child-centered programs are designed to connect with the life experience and developmental level of the child while presenting information about the Catholic Christian tradition. Commendable as this is, children can experience religious instruction as separate and removed from the Sunday liturgical celebration, and vice versa. One way to bring the two together would be the integration of lectionary readings into traditional programs of religious education.

Some religious educators are questioning the effectiveness of traditional programs of religious education in parishes today. They have based their objections in part on the lack of focus and inadequate content found in many of these traditional programs. Older and more traditional ways of doing catechesis seem to be foundering in a sea of construction paper, glue sticks, and fill-in-the-blanks. Catechists appear to be more concerned with classroom management than with the faith of those they are attempting to manage. As Robert Duggan and Maureen Kelly insist in *The Christian Initiation of Children: Hope for the Future* (New York: Paulist Press, 1991, p. 11) "the enterprise of religious education is undergoing a time of turbulence." They maintain that religious education as we know it today just doesn't work. One aspect of their solution would be to focus exclusively on the lectionary as the source of both content and methodology for catechesis of elementary-age children. Perhaps a more prudent, and some would say more acceptable, approach would be to integrate existing catechetical programs with what goes on on Sundays at Mass. The lectionary is certainly worth a try.

***TIME OUT!

Once again you are invited to think about what you have been reading. Please consider the following questions, either on your own or with another person.

1. What deficiencies or inadequacies are you aware of in your catechetical program?

2. How do you think these inadequacies might be addressed?

3. What is your catechetical "Hope for the Future"?

A Brief History of Catechesis

Young Maria, in "The Sound of Music," sings that "Nothing comes from nothing, nothing ever could . . ." The present reality of catechetics certainly did not "come from nothing," but rather from out of its own historical development. The historical precedent for lectionary-based catechesis is found within the ancient initiation or catechumenal process. Religious education, too, has had "a long past but a short history," as Mary Boys states in *Biblical Interpretation in Religious Education* (Birmingham: Religious Education Press, 1980, p. 278). A brief encounter with the short history of catechetics in this century might be helpful in understanding where we have come thus far in our attempts to reach beyond what we have been doing to what we might be doing in the future.

The scholastic or indoctrination system of catechisms and rote learning so prevalent in the first half of the twentieth century will be addressed in some detail in the next chapter. Many of us well remember the impact of the Baltimore Catechism on the practice of religious education. This method finally gave way during the 1960's in the United States to a scripture-based approach where *Heilsgeschichte* (Josef Jungmann's "all-embracing salvific plan of God") formed the basis for content. For the first time in contemporary catechetical history, scripture, not doctrine, became the primary focus of religious education content.

"Salvation history" was no longer confined to doctrinal statements included in catechisms, but rather was rediscovered in the story of our faith, in scripture. The proclamation of the faith (the kerygma) became the content. The kerygmatic approach to catechesis called for the use of scripture, the inclusion of liturgy, and the exposure to Christian witness along with the doctrine. Mary Boys writes with enormous wisdom and scholarship of the issues surrounding this approach in *Biblical Interpretation in Religious Education*. Her analysis of the rise and fall of the salvation history/kerygmatic approach indicates clearly its impact on contemporary religious education: "Salvation history, as the centripetal force in the kerygmatic movement in twentieth century Catholicism, functioned to renew church life, to invite and to introduce people to the study of Scripture, and to draw together the biblical, liturgical, and catechetical movements" (p. 126). In short, the kerygmatic approach broke open a whole new way of doing catechesis, and after that nothing has been quite the same.

Once it became evident that there was more to catechesis than the learning of doctrine, the discoveries of Jean Piaget, Erik Erikson, Ronald Goldman, Lawrence Kohlberg, James Fowler, and others who studied human growth and development began to be appropriated into catechetical methodology. Scientific investigations revealed what parents have always known: children grow and develop in certain patterns and will only learn what and when they are ready to learn. There is no hurrying of the process. Religious education textbooks began to reflect this insight by developing scope-and-sequence charts aimed at respecting the learning capacity of the child and by including such sections as "characteristics of a nine-year-old" for the edification of catechists who did not happen to live with a nine-year-old child. Educational methodology used in "secular" education already recognized the importance of teaching according to the developmental level of the child, but this was a new thing for Catholic religious education programs. At last the experts gave catechists the permission to do what often came naturally: no more ten commandments in the first grade, no more lengthy treatises on the nature of salvation for seventh-graders, no more lists of sins in the second grade. This was progress indeed.

Coupled with the developmental psychologists and their discoveries about how children grow in moral reasoning, faith, and religion readiness, new insights began to emerge concerning the role of families and religious institutions in enabling and encouraging that growth. John Westerhoff has emerged as a strong voice articulating the importance of traditions, practices, and rituals in the handing on of the faith. Westerhoff's "socialization" approach maintains that effective religious education occurs primarily in communities of faith, especially families, that are attempting to live out their tradition and to express that tradition liturgically. His insightful and (at the time) original examination of these issues appeared in his now-classic *Will Our Children Have Faith?* (New York: Seabury Press, 1976).

Westerhoff expands his arguments in his article "Catechetics: An Anglican Perspective" in *Sourcebook for Modern Catechetics* (Michael Warren, ed., Winona: St. Mary's Press, 1983) and states that catechesis not only "acknowledges that we are enculturated or socialized within a community of memory and vision" but also "challenges the community to be morally responsible for both the ways in which it aids persons to live in community and for the ways by which it influences the lives of others." It is "incumbent upon the community of faith to accept responsibility for disciplined, intentional, and faithful life together."

It is clear, then, that the role of the community in forming faith as well as in expressing it cannot be underestimated. People come to faith as they participate in the lived experience of the community, as God becomes evident to them in the persons, places, and events of their everyday lives. The emphasis on an appreciation for the importance of life experience in catechesis has its roots in the early works of Alfonso Nebreda (*Kerygma in Crisis?* Chicago: Loyola Press, 1965) and Gabriel Moran (*Theology of Revelation,* and *Catechesis of Revelation,* New York: Herder and Herder, 1966). Building on Vatican II's "Dei Verbum," the Constitution on Divine Revelation, both Nebreda and Moran maintain that the most effective catechesis is that which develops out of the ordinary experiences of life. God is revealed not only in "created realities," in Jesus Christ, in the Holy Spirit, and in the Church, but is also "manifested" (the term used by The National Catechetical Directory in #51) in the daily lives of people of faith. Therefore, life experience has the potential for offering profound insight into the nature of God when one's experience is considered in the light of the faith tradition of the community. This concept of experiential catechesis has been described very clearly in the work of Thomas Groome.

Thomas Groome's theory of experiential catechesis, "Shared Christian Praxis," is a theologically sound yet pastoral methodology that respects the importance of one's life experience in coming to know God. In Groome's *Christian Religious Education* (San Francisco: Harper and Row, 1980) he proposed a "kingdom-centered" approach to religious education that was a far cry from the "saving your soul" mentality of some previous religious education methodologies. As Groome writes on page 50: "The Kingdom of God invites a response of constant conversion. . . . That inner conversion must turn us outward toward God in our neighbor. This love requires, in turn, that as individuals we strive to live justly and for justice, peacefully and for peace, equally and for equality; that we live by and promote the values of the Kingdom, God's will for the world."

Groome's "Shared Christian Praxis" methodology makes it possible to lead people to a faith response that can result in a conversion that will bring about the reign of God: peace, justice, and equality. Groome's five-step process begins with bringing to mind one's life experience and then allowing reflection on that life experience to occur. Only then is the "Church teaching" that is relevant to the life experience offered as a way to assist in the understanding of the meaning of that experience. Further reflection is encouraged so that both Church teaching and the experience might be integrated in an attempt to bring about a faith response that indeed is centered on the values of God's reign: peace, justice, and equality.

In this methodology, the process of religious education (Groome's preferred terminology) assumes a more holistic stance: Church teaching is not isolated from life experience, but rather is presented alongside it. The faith response called for comes more authentically because it is connected to what is known, to what has been experienced, and it makes sense. It is hard to ignore the call of God to peace, justice, and equality when our experience has shown us what this means. It is easier to ignore Church teaching that comes out of a theological vacuum. Groome and others such as Robert Hater insist, then, that all theology and Church teaching is best developed and understood as it comes into relationship with life experience, and that connecting life experience with the experience of God is vital before religious education can make sense.

Catechesis in this century has moved through many stages and phases: from catechism to kerygmatic to developmental to socialization and finally to an experiential approach. Now we are becoming aware of the significance of the catechetical approach used for Christian initiation that is strongly focused on lectionary readings. It is important to view lectionary-based catechesis for children as an extension of many of these historical catechetical developments. Lectionary-based catechesis for children incorporates scripture, liturgy, and effective and professional methodology that respects developmental levels. Most important, all of this is presented within the context of the community of faith. Before going on to some specific ways in which lectionary-based catechesis can actually be experienced, why not take some . . .

***TIME OUT!

Here are some more questions for you to consider, either alone or with someone else.

1. How can you honestly answer the question "Will our children have faith?" In your opinion, what would be the most effective way to bring about an affirmative answer?

2. What part has your own life experience played in "teaching" you about God, Church, and your faith traditions?

3. What is your role in "salvation history"?

Family or Intergenerational Catechesis

At present there are many variations on the theme of "lectionary-based catechesis." As catechetical leaders and thinkers recognize some of the deficiencies of more traditional "classroom" approaches, there is an increasing motivation to look beyond instructional models of catechesis to try to discover how the faith tradition can be handed on in other ways. As always, we continue to look back at how catechesis has developed to see where it might go.

John Westerhoff's ideas give us a clue. He recognizes that families, however they are defined, are primary communicators of faith. Might it be that lectionary-based catechesis could find its most comfortable home within the family setting?

The family-centered or intergenerational approach to lectionary-based catechesis presents some exciting possibilities. In this variation, entire families including extended family members can be engaged in at-home catechetical sessions focused on the Sunday readings. Parents, as the primary religious educators of their children, are usually responsible for these sessions held around the kitchen table or in the park or back yard under a tree. Many creative new authors and publishers have developed reams of materials for use in these family settings. Parents are encouraged to learn and prepare themselves to utilize these materials and to work with their children by participating in programs aimed at promoting parenting skills, catechist formation, or adult scripture-study-and-prayer programs in their parish or diocese. They then have the unique oppurtunity to hand on their faith to their children in the time-honored way, through example guided by informed faith.

This description of parental involvement in the faith life of their children evokes an idealistic image of happy families eagerly reading scripture together and living out what they have heard in charitable acts toward others. Anyone who has ever raised children can easily see what's wrong with this picture, but there is no doubt that this approach is one that should be assisted, supported, and encouraged by pastors, parish staffs, and catechetical leaders. As difficult as it might be at times for family members to communicate with each other, this non-threatening context for family conversation might be just what is needed to facilitate intergenerational understanding.

The catalysts in this process, in many cases, turn out to be those people loosely described as the "intergenerational" ones: the grandparents, extended family members, and friends, neighbors or fellow-parishioners who join with the nuclear family for these sessions. The mixture of young and old and in-between enables a certain courtesy, politeness and openness to differences not always present in the dynamic of Mom and/or Dad and the kids. As we well know, in today's world the expectation that families consist only of Mom and Dad and the kids is not always realistic. Lectionary-based catechesis acknowledges new family definitions and structures that include single parents, merged families with all the attendant multi-grandparents or siblings that are his-hers-and-ours, or the person who is single by choice, divorce, separation, or death of a spouse. The renewed image of family can and often does include a mixture of all of the above, and the Sunday lectionary readings provide the common experience out of which all members of the group can have the opportunity to form their personal and communal response.

John Westerhoff describes the potential for creative change that is found in intergenerational catechesis based on liturgical celebration in *A Faithful Church* (Wilton, CN: Morehouse-Barlow, 1981, p. 296):

> With the reform of the Sunday liturgy into a family-oriented, participating, communal celebration of word and sacrament, there is a renewed interest in the relationship of learning and liturgy. In many churches the Sunday School is being transformed into an intergenerational preparation for the Sunday Eucharist based upon an experience of and reflection upon the lectionary texts.

However, Westerhoff cautions that this experience not become merely a "community of nurture" that neglects "proclamation, conversions, transformations, and new beginnings." Westerhoff admits that while the "process of catechesis necessarily takes place within an intergenerational community of faith" it is vital to know that "the community which is at the heart of catechesis is a gift, a miracle, a grace." He insists there can be no turning inward or ignoring of the need to reach out, to evangelize, to share with others this gift, miracle, grace. The family, however it is defined, can be an ideal medium through which catechesis can be experienced, both in the giving and in the receiving.

The liturgical experience to which people of all ages have access can be, then, a sound basis for catechesis. The Liturgy of the Word speaks to us all. Catechetical sessions based on the Sunday lectionary readings can be valuable for both adults and children, however they are designed or presented. One key to success is the willingness of the intergenerational group to prioritize time and energy to this project, and this allocation of precious resources can be encouraged through liturgical experiences that truly enable full, active, and conscious participation on the part of the entire assembly. Homilies need careful thought and preparation if they are to appeal to many ages: a nearly impossible task, my priest friends tell me, but certainly one worth pursuing. Music must be appropriate and singable, readings must be proclaimed clearly in a reasonably good acoustical space, and the bread and wine and candles and water and incense must be recognizable for what they are and for what they mean.

When all of this comes together in liturgies that speak, people of all ages listen and respond.

Liturgy of the Word for Children: Ritual, Not Catechesis

Liturgy of the Word for children has been misunderstood by many as another way of doing lectionary-based catechesis. This misinterpretation is probably the result of an admirable eagerness on the part of catechists to use every opportunity available to bring children to faith, including the time during Sunday Mass when children are exposed to their own version of the Liturgy of the Word. However worthy the intentions might be, the prevailing view by both liturgists and catechists is that Liturgy of the Word for children should not be a time for formal catechesis at all, but rather should be seen as an extension or continuation of the liturgical experience. The question of what Liturgy of the Word for children actually is, or should be, is one that perhaps can be best answered if we take a brief look at how the Liturgy of the Word for children is best celebrated within the Sunday liturgical experience.

The celebration of the Liturgy of the Word for children has its roots in the "Christian Initiation of Children Who Have Reached Catechetical Age," in Part II of the Order of Christian Initiation of Adults. In preparing children for initiation, they are dismissed or "sent forth" from Mass to a place set aside for them, as the adults are, to reflect on the Word of God and to be further catechized while the Liturgy of the Eucharist is going on back in church. Adults are present with the entire assembly for the Liturgy of the Word, and are blessed and sent forth following the homily. With the children, however, it soon became evident that a more effective experience of the Word could be accomplished if the children were exposed to the simplified readings from the Lectionary for Children and if the homily was geared to their level of understanding. So, rather than listening to the "adult" readings and homily, the children preparing for initiation began to be sent forth from Mass after the opening prayers to celebrate their own Liturgy of the Word. The children, as did the adult catechumens who were sent forth after the "adult" homily, then remained in the place set aside for them during the rest of Mass (and even beyond) for formal catechetical sessions based on the lectionary readings.

For baptized children who have received eucharist, however, the experience of Liturgy of the Word is quite different in its intention.

These children are sent forth to hear the Word of God proclaimed in a manner suitable to their comprehension and response, just as do children preparing for initiation. However, children who are part of the eucharistic assembly return to the assembly following their Liturgy of the Word and continue their participation in the eucharistic liturgy.

So it is not surprising that in some parishes the process of the Liturgy of the Word became confused with a process for catechesis. In the beginning, the children were "dismissed" from Mass by announcing sometime after the opening prayer that "it's time for the children to leave now," and the children trotted merrily out of church. They trotted merrily back into church at some point during the collection, waving colorful construction paper or crayoned works of art, the creation of which seemed to have been the purpose of their dismissal. This is indeed not what Liturgy of the Word for children is all about. As we will see, the Liturgy of the Word for children is a liturgical, not a catechetical experience, a ritual that is part of Mass for them.

However, the celebration of the Liturgy of the Word for children also developed in response to several needs, not the least of which is the need for adults to hear and respond to the Word without the distraction of wriggling, bored children armed with *My Picture Book of Saints,* pencil stubs from the collection envelope niche, and bulletins on which to draw. It has always been evident that young children are less than engrossed in the readings at Mass, and are especially difficult to engage during the homily. When presented well, the Liturgy of the Word for children attempts to bring children to a level of participation appropriate for them and to enable them to celebrate this ritual in a meaningful and prayerful ways.

At the same time, though, it must be clearly understood that participation in the Liturgy of the Word for children in no way hints that the children are not welcome at Mass. To the contrary: while this portion of the liturgical celebration is special for them and is geared to their own level of spiritual and intellectual growth, they return to their families to continue the Liturgy of the Eucharist where full participation consists of communion with the entire assembly as they all pray, give thanks, and eat and drink together. The children greatly enhance the community of faith as they join in the eucharistic activities, having already been "fed" by the Word in ways that are meaningful to them.

In parishes where the Liturgy of the Word is indeed a meaningful experience for the children, as well as for the adults, a definite sense of unity is present. When children arrive at the church for Sunday liturgy, ideally with their families, they along with the entire assembly participate in the opening prayers and penitential rites. The children are then called forward by the presider, blessed, and invited to process with their catechist (holding the lectionary on high) from the church to the place set aside for them. Often, the entire assembly sings the children out of church with a simple antiphon.

In the place prepared for them, the readings are proclaimed, the psalm response and alleluia are sung, and the reflection on the Word is led by the catechist/presider. Every effort is made to insure that this time away from the adult assembly is a continuation of the liturgical ritual, which means that paper-flower or coloring-book activity is not appropriate. The children are led by the catechist/presider to discover within the readings what they will discover, keeping in mind that the nature of their insight will obviously depend on age and developmental levels.

The catechist/presider enables response from the children in several ways. The Lectionary for Children, which presents readings that have been shortened but not changed, is used: no proclamations of the entire ninth chapter of John's gospel on the Fourth Sunday of Lent, no matter how tempted the catechist/presider might be. The second reading is often omitted. The homiletic focus is on dialogue and participation, with questions that allow the children freedom to answer without fear of "getting it wrong." The session ends with a shortened version of the Creed, and the children process back into the church during the collection basket pause or while the music preceding the preparation of the gifts is sung.

The entire process usually lasts around 20 to 30 minutes, and is fraught with potential for confusion: space limitations, priest-presiders who "forget" about dismissing and blessing the children, children's places in church taken over by late-arriving adults, the hustle and bustle of the returning children as they seek their parents and try to get into those occupied seats. However, creative approaches are possible. Fr. David Sork, pastor of St. Louis of France Church in La Puente, California, reports that because of standing room only at Sunday Masses in his mega-parish, "the children on their return come and sit in the sanctuary—around 200 of them!"

In parishes where the celebration of the Liturgy of the Word for children is done creatively, simply, and successfully there is a great sense of wonder and delight on the part of parents, children, catechists, pastors, and the entire assembly. An actual experience of the Word of God takes place as children are led prayerfully to *listen* and to *respond.* Opportunities abound for family members to compare notes later on about the readings they have all heard proclaimed in different ways. The catechists/presiders grow in their appreciation of scripture as they prayerfully prepare for Sunday morning. The entire liturgical year, not just the school year, is experienced: these sessions don't begin in September and end in June, just as the celebration of Mass is not limited to the school year time frame. Children at last are intentionally and consistenly exposed to all those wonderful readings during the "green season" of ordinary time in the summer. Those in the assembly who have no children are usually charmed and warmed to see the young people processing in and out and quickly come to expect this as part of the Sunday ritual. And pastors appreciate the chance to prepare and deliver homilies that can touch the minds and hearts of adults without concern that the children in the assembly will be left out.

The concern for liturgists is that these sessions will be misused and turned into catechetical sessions with over-eager catechists who will attempt to present an entire grade-level class during this time, complete with lecture, messy art activities, and music with gestures. Liturgy of the Word for children should be understood as exactly that: Liturgy of the Word. This is not a time for formal catechesis, but rather for children to experience within a *liturgical* setting the Word of God. Whatever catechesis occurs is catechesis that would occur within the framework of the Liturgy of the Word anyway, if that particular Liturgy of the Word were presented to an assembly of children. Some creative ideas, good advice, and of course a few cautions concerning ways to do this well are found in paragraphs 41–49 of the *Directory on Children's Masses,* a postconciliar document issued by the Sacred Congregation for Divine Worship in 1973 but still quite helpful.

So it is clear why the Liturgy of the Word for children is not included in a generic explanation or description of lectionary-based catechesis, although many of the same principles certainly apply in both cases. The ritual of the Liturgy of the Word must be honored and respected at all times, and if catechesis occurs it is not an intentionally designed outcome of the liturgical experience.

However, there is indeed a vital connection between Liturgy of the Word for children and lectionary-based catechesis, and we certainly do not want to miss it. When children experience their own Liturgy of the Word, presented in comfortable settings using language they can easily understand and allowing them to respond verbally to what they have heard, catechesis both before and after the liturgy takes on a whole new meaning. The children remember those readings, and come to amazing new understandings when they hear and listen at their own level. Whatever a catechist presents to them in the actual catechetical setting at a later time is enhanced by this liturgical experience. The connection between the liturgical experience and the classroom experience is clear, and the children can view the catechetical experience as one which relates to what they did at Mass on Sunday. Without this connection, both the liturgical experience and the catechetical experience can seem isolated from one another, with little in common. One of our major goals in lectionary-based catechesis, of course, is to bring the two together. It is clear, then, that the clue to the relationship between Liturgy of the Word for children and lectionary-based catechesis is found in how both experiences are presented and inter-related by the catechists involved.

Having made that point, it is necessary to make a brief comment about the role of the catechist/presider at the Liturgy of the Word for children. It is clear that this person is not simply a catechist, but rather enjoys a dual role that includes that of presider at a liturgical celebration. However, in most parishes the people who would ask to participate in this activity are often those engaged in catechetical ministry. It is important that a distinction be made between how one catechizes in a formal, intentional, and systematic way and how one presides at a liturgical celebration. The catechist/presider needs to be well prepared to lead this liturgical celebration with the children: the scripture passages are studied, prayed, and examined and a brief homiletic response is planned. Commentaries are consulted and exegesis is done just as when actual catechetical sessions are being designed. But in this case, the catechist/presider does not lay out a specific course of study or lesson plan of any kind. The presider role takes over, and the ritual stands on its own. The readings, sung responses, and dialogue homily are all part of the ritual that began in church with the entire assembly and that continues when the children return to the assembly. The catechist/presider enables the children to pray, to respond, and to participate fully in the ritual.

In a wonderful and insightful book *A Child Shall Lead Them: A Guide to Celebrating the Word with Children* (Loveland, OH: Treehaus Publications, 1992), authors Gerard A. Pottebaum, Paule Freeburg, and Joyce Kelleher describe in great detail the process of leading children to prayer through the Liturgy of the Word. Along with many many sound and practical ideas for implementing this process, the authors describe "the leader" (or using my language, the "catechist/presider") as the one who is "not a classroom teacher or babysitter, as significant as those services are in other settings. The leader's primary task is to awaken in children a sense of God's presence in the word proclaimed and in the Word made flesh in their lives, to open the hearts of children to God's word and nurture their response in prayer, praise and Christian living" (pp. 30–31). So the catechist/presider is formed for this role by acquiring sound exegetical skills combined with a certain catechetical expertise which not only respects the spiritual and developmental capabilities of the children but that also is expressed in the ability to speak of one's own experience of God with conviction, sincerity, and enthusiasm.

***TIME OUT!

Please think about what you've been reading and complete the following statements, either on your own or with another person.

1. The scripture passage or story that is most familiar to me is_____.

2. I remember this passage or story because_____.

3. In this passage or story, it seems that God is portrayed as_____.

4. This scripture passage or story makes me feel_____.

Lectionary-Based Catechesis as a Supplement to Existing Programs

A final aspect of lectionary-based catechesis needs to be examined at length, and that is the main purpose of this book. As we proceed through the following chapters, we will take a look at ways in which lectionary-based catechesis affects and is affected by traditional child-centered, curriculum-based catechetical programs. For now, it might be enough to briefly describe some of the ways in which lectionary-based catechesis is already happening in some of these programs.

Because of the difficulties mentioned previously concerning the implementation of the Liturgy of the Word for children, most especially difficulties surrounding logistics and adequate facilities, many parishes are attempting as best they can to honor the principles of lectionary-based catechesis in designing catechetical programs. Some catechetical leaders are advising catechists to present the Sunday scripture readings to the children before, during, or after the regular catechetical session, with the intention of exposing them one way or the other to God's Word.

One DRE I know has developed a creative idea in her parish catechetical program: all the children are gathered in the church before their class time, the readings are proclaimed and responses are sung, there is a brief homily given by one of the catechists or by the DRE herself, and the children are dismissed to their grade-level classrooms. It is hoped and suggested that the catechists will build upon this introduction in their time with the children, but this remains merely a suggestion.

In many parish schools, lectionary readings for the forthcoming Sunday are part of the Friday religion class. In some places, "Father" comes to class to do these readings and to present a short homily. The children are given the opportunity to enjoy a sneak preview of the Sunday readings with the hope that they will be more motivated to listen carefully and pay attention when they celebrate Mass on Sunday.

Another spin on this idea has the readings proclaimed prayerfully in ritual fashion during Monday's religion class. This follows more accurately the format that makes the Liturgy of the Word for children an authentic liturgical experience. In a sense the Sunday experience is re-created in school on Mondays, with the added attraction of room and time for dialogue, reflection, and opportunities for further response in prayer, song, and even some of those paper-flower activities.

Other ways of integrating lectionary-based catechesis with traditional catechetical programs arrived on the scene as some publishers of traditional religion texts produced (sometimes rather hurriedly) materials that corresponded to their previous grade-level school-year curricula but with the inclusion of the Sunday readings in each lesson. This could be a step in the right direction, certainly, but seems to be a neither-fish-nor-fowl approach.

Other publishers went further with entirely new curricula based on the three lectionary cycles, containing elaborate lesson plans corresponding to the readings for each Sunday throughout the year. In both cases the classroom-centered programs continue to offer the usual catechetical process respecting life experience, doctrinal content, and faith response, with lots of art activities, fill-in-the-blanks, and suggestions for supplementary videos and storybooks. These materials, while in many ways excellent resources, at times appear to attempt to do too much.

This brief review and overview of lectionary-based catechesis as it is present today in our catechetical world reminds us that, as always, there is no one way to "do" catechesis. However, this newest approach is also the oldest approach, and perhaps we need to be aware of the need to look to sacred scripture for the method and content of our catechetical endeavors much more closely than we have been accustomed to doing in the past. How can we do this effectively? What can a catechist expect to accomplish by putting more emphasis on the Sunday readings and the liturgical cycle? Read on.

And here are some more resources for you . . .

Bernstein, Eleanor, ed. *Children in the Assembly of the Church.* Chicago: Liturgy Training Publications, 1992.

Flannery, Austin. *Vatican Council II: The Conciliar and Post Conciliar Documents.* Collegeville, MN: Liturgical Press, 1984.

Osborne, Kenan B. *The Christian Sacraments of Initiation.* New York: Paulist Press, 1987.

Pottebaum, Gerard, Freeburg, Paule, and Kelleher, Joyce. *A Child Shall Lead Them.* Loveland, OH: Treehaus Publications, 1992.

The Rite of Christian Initiation of Adults, U.S. edition. Chicago: Liturgy Training Publications, 1988.

Westerhoff, John. *A Faithful Church: Issues in the History of Catechesis.* Wilton, CN: Morehouse-Barlow, 1981.

Wilde, James A., ed. *When Should We Confirm?* Chicago: Liturgy Training Publications, 1989.

3

Traditional Catechesis:
Educating Catholics in the Faith

Catechisms and Catechesis

Now that we have examined the development of lectionary-based catechesis and its close relationship to liturgical celebration, perhaps we need to clarify further the importance of catechesis in implementing this newest approach. This might best be done within the context of where we have come from in our catechetical journeys, and then to take a look at where we might be going in the future. Catechesis as we know it today is a complex and sometimes puzzling endeavor. It was not always that way, or so it seemed to me when I was "growing up Catholic."

Those of us "Cradle Catholics" who are of a certain age remember vividly the religion lessons of our youth. One by one, row by row, we were required to recite the memorized answers to the questions put to us by the Baltimore Catechism. The same Catechism questions were memorized over and over each year, and like all good Catholics of my era I can still recite that a "sacrament is an outward sign instituted by Christ to give grace," although it has taken me many years of adult study and reflection to find meaning in that statement and to realize its inadequacy. At any rate, early on in my Catholic school days I discovered a way to avoid having to carefully memorize *all* the answers assigned for homework. I always sat several seats back from the front of the class, and it was simple to figure out which questions would be answered by those in the row ahead of me. Sister always assigned the questions in turn, and so unless someone really failed to recite correctly (a nearly inconceivable occurence—Sister was very persuasive in her ability to convince us to learn those answers) I could usually predict which question would fall to me to answer, and I would fiercely concentrate my powers of memory on that one while the others were reciting. By such creative maneuvering a future catechist was made.

It certainly was not an ideal system, and yet I survived to go into my mid-life years enormously curious about the nature of God, Church, and my own destiny. Could there have been a seed of interest planted in that sterile soil of memorized theology? Could it be that the buried seed began to germinate years later when the answers I learned became questions for me?

The educational or pedagogical theory—if there was such an intention—that supported the Baltimore Catechism question-and-answer method was that memorized information would surface at a time when it became relevant in the life of the learner. Many Catholic adults today insist on the correctness of that theory. They can recite, in unison, that "God made me to know him, to love him, and to serve him in this world and to be happy with him forever in the next." Some things that are learned as a child are never forgotten, like riding a bicycle or the rules of Kick the Can. It would seem that once adults begin to look for meaning and significance in riding a bike or in defining "sacrament" or in a statement expressing the meaning of one's existence, those remembered skills and ideas become at least a starting point for mature application and further discovery and growth.

The obvious fly in the Baltimore Catechism ointment, however, was not just the methodology. The technique of memorization seems to get all the bad press whenever the "Baltimore" is mentioned, but contemporary catechetical theory does not view memorized learning as something always to be avoided. To the contrary, formal prayers, some scripture passages, creedal statements and verbal responses during liturgical celebrations are all taught carefully throughout a child's life. Repetition is an effective aid to real learning, and poetry, songs, lilting prayer responses, and consistent review of some key theological concepts can certainly be an effective part of the catechetical experience.

Having said that, it probably goes without saying that the memorized question-and-answer methodology when used exclusively most certainly lacks pedagogical and catechetical acceptance today. However, a more critical look at the Baltimore Catechism as it existed in my youth reveals weaknesses other than those found in its methodology, most notably the limited and simplistic explanations of deep and profound theological concepts and the equal treatment of all matters throughout the book. In an essay in Michael Warren's *Sourcebook for Modern Catechetics* (St. Mary's Press, 1983) Sr. Mary Charles Bryce writes of the many criticisms of the catechism when it was introduced in various dioceses after it was published in 1885:

The catechism was theologically weak on many scores: the brevity of its treatment of God and the angels, the absence of any consideration of divine providence, only one question about the resurrection—a reference to the day it happened rather than to the significance of the event—and insufficient attention to the Holy Spirit.

This essay by Sr. Mary Charles, originally published as "Happy Birthday Baltimore Catechism" in *Catechist* magazine in April, 1972, seems particularly relevant today with the publication of *The Catechism of the Catholic Church* and as its full impact on the catechetical community is yet to be felt.

While the question-and-answer format is missing from *The Catechism of the Catholic Church,* Mary Charles Bryce's criticism of the Baltimore Catechism alluding to the "stunting of thought processes involved in (giving) complete answers and . . . the monotony of the entire text which gave equal treatment to all matters" might well be aimed at this newest catechism also. The disadvantage of all catechisms is that they by nature do not provoke inquiry and of course limit the imaginative quest for further insight and understanding. For that reason alone, professional religious educators today are somewhat uneasy about the entry of the *Catechism* into the contemporary catechetical scene.

However, in his presentation "Overview: The Catechism of the Catholic Church" (reprinted in *Origins,* Vol. 23, No. 1, May 20, 1993) to those gathered at the National Conference of Catechetical Leadership in April, 1993, Fr. John Pollard from the Department of Education, U.S. Catholic Conference defends, defines, and explains the role of *The Catechism of the Catholic Church:*

> The catechism is a resource, a point of reference. It is not directly intended for use by children and youth. It is a reference book. It belongs in the reference section of one's library, along with a theological dictionary, a biblical commentary, and the documents of the Second Vatican Council.

As such, the *Catechism* is intended primarily "for bishops as teachers of the faith and pastors of the church." Also, authors, editors, and publishers of catechetical materials "will have to consider the catechism carefully in the revision of their current materials . . . just as they have depended on other important church documents in the past." The *Catechism* contains no pedagogical or methodological suggestions, but will depend on the cultural and developmental context of those using it as the reference it is intended to be. Instead, Pollard insists that the *Catechism* is "a means to achieve religious literacy. It is not the container of religious literacy. Religious literacy consists in the assimilation of religious knowledge, not just the accumulation of religious knowledge."

Preliminary evaluation of *The Catechism of the Catholic Church* indicates a certain unevenness in the presentation of its doctrinal content. Fr. Gerald Sloyan, speaking to participants at a conference on the *Catechism* in May, 1993 at The Catholic University of America, mentioned some difficulties he finds in the use of scripture throughout the volume. Sloyan is concerned about biblical literalism, a lack of ecumenical sensitivity (the Old Testament is treated as a preparation for Christ rather than as the people Israel chosen by God in their own right), and the use of proof-texting. He points out that not until paragraph #2653 (out of the 2,865 numbered paragraphs) are Catholics told they should read the Bible. Even then, there is more emphasis on how not to use the Bible than on how to use it.

At this same conference Fr. Robert Friday investigated "Conscience Formation in the Catechism" and also found a lack of consistency. In Section Two, which addresses the sacraments, the context for morality is presented as being found within the community and in its celebration of the Christian mystery. However, in Section Three covering the commandments the context for morality is found to be in following the law, and there is the implication that conscience is formed by learning the expectations of the law. Fr. Friday wonders if "there are different hands at work here." Of course there are, since at this time the identities of the authors of the *Catechism* are unknown and committee work often results in contradictions. Fr. Friday describes even further inconsistencies. The *Catechism* states in #1975 that Jesus' law of love is the cornerstone of moral teaching and that love frees us from legalism. But the whole presentation of morality within the document seems to be continuing the legalistic processes of early centuries, especially in the "commandments" section.

However, progress *is* being made! The Baltimore Catechism did not even mention conscience other than to teach about what an "examination of conscience" is: ". . . a sincere effort to call to mind all the sins we have committed since our last confession" and how to do it: ". . . by calling to mind the commandments of God and of the Church, and by asking ourselves how we may have sinned with regard to them." The concept of the possibility of forming a conscience beyond the keeping of commandments was not considered. In contrast, catechetical materials today refer to conscience as involving choice and judgment. The *This Is Our Faith* Grade Four text published by Silver Burdett Ginn (1991), for instance, defines conscience as "our power to judge whether something is good or bad" and states that "Making choices between good and bad is not always easy. But our conscience helps us to know whether something is good or bad. . . . Our conscience may guide us. . . . At times we are not sure of what we should do. . . . The Holy Spirit guides our conscience to help us choose what is good."

The Catechism of the Catholic Church in #1783 states that "we must not act against an informed conscience," an ancient teaching of the church and a tradition held sacred through the ages. The Baltimore Catechism didn't speak of a conscience that could be informed other than by adherence to the commandments. Yet believers will always know in their hearts that there is more to understanding the nature of God and of God's mercy than what is contained in catechisms or in classroom teaching. We learn to "choose what is good" in many ways: by assimilation of knowledge, by watching and listening to our experience, and by the grace of God present in those who model faith for us.

So we see that in spite of some obvious flaws *The Catechism of the Catholic Church* certainly has its merits as a resource for thinking Catholics and as a source of common language to be used in describing and defining doctrinal positions. Publishers of religious education materials must comply with the content of the *Catechism* as the norm for the content of children's catechesis. Creative catechists, as they have always done, will unpack the content of this document and will design methodologies that successfully link its content with life experience. Themes in the *Catechism* echo themes found in the lectionary readings, and the *Catechism* provides another resource for catechists to use in handing on the message of salvation in authentic yet meaningful and exciting ways.

The human inadequacies of the *Catechism,* particularly obvious in the inconsistencies and contradictions, in some ways could be seen as a microcosm of the Church as divine but all too human institution throughout the ages. We who are Church, we who are the people of God, are still not God. But God is with us, in our Church institutions and in our own humanity, and we can be sure of God's continuing presence even as documents are composed that try to express our limited understanding of the mystery of faith.

***TIME OUT!

Once again you are invited to reflect about what you've been reading and to consider these questions.

1. If you were "raised" on the Baltimore Catechism, what question/ answer combination has stayed with you? Can you define this question/answer in your own words?

2. If you were not "raised" on the Baltimore Catechism, what memorized portion of the Creed or of a favorite prayer has obscure meaning for you? Can you put it into your own words?

3. What is your definition of "conscience"? Where did you acquire your own definition? Cite your source!

Catechesis and Catechists

And so, like the Baltimore Catechism, successful integration of *The Catechism of the Catholic Church* into the faith life of young Catholics will depend greatly on how it is presented and used. Again, the lived faith of the catechists who unpack this "rich resource" of common Catholic belief will make the "intellectual content of the faith" come alive for the children. It is always the catechists—more than content, more than catechetical resources, more than apostolic constitutions—who bring the added dimension of personal faith into their catechetical sessions. Catechists "make sense" out of the intellectual content of Catholic belief as they find creative ways to express creed, commandment, worship, and prayer, and in this way truly bring children to faith.

Catechisms throughout the history of the church have depended on catechists to interpret and connect theological discourse within the parameters of the life experience of those coming to faith. When I was a fifth-grader concentrating so diligently on memorizing a catechism answer, waiting my turn to stand and recite, I was not concerned about the meaning of that answer. The whole process was just something that happened in school, that I took for granted as part of "religion class."

But there were other components of "religion class" that did have meaning for me, most of all in the person of the one who taught me. Many would agree that I was taught *about* my religion as I learned the contents of the Baltimore Catechism, over and over. But because I was blessed in those years to be taught by some women who modeled the best of religious life (and I can truly laugh with love at "Nunsense" or "Sister Act" because of them) there was much more to it. Surely those good and kind nuns who taught me "shared their faith" as they saw to it that I learned a lot of what I considered to be inconsequential stuff. I saw holiness in them, and I watched and observed and assimilated their attitudes of patience, good humor, and strength. They seemed to take great joy in their work, they prayed beautifully, and they affirmed for me what I was beginning to think God was like.

My fifth grade teacher, Sister Mary Alice, was indeed one who shared her faith, who showed me by her example and modeling just what a good and even holy woman was like. She was very patient, very affirming, and she told good stories. She even laughed with us from time to time—although in looking back I'm sure she believed in the ancient wisdom of all elementary teachers that you "never smile before Christmas" if you want to maintain good discipline in the classroom. I was enormously impressed by the way she prayed. Even though there was a great deal of emphasis in those days on formal prayer, and "Sister" did that well (not even having to look at the words of the Act of Faith in the back of the catechism), she also was the first person I had ever experienced who prayed spontaneously and really seemed to be conversing with God.

There was indeed something different about this teacher who personified the concept of "catechist" for me. Without recalling specifically how she did it, my fifth grade teacher brought her faith to me, offered it with a smile, and challenged me to accept it and make it mine.

I'm sure "Sister" also did her best to explain the meaning of some of those catechism questions and answers to us. I'm sure she must have defined words, used examples, and interpreted the obscure concepts and language of the Baltimore Catechism. I'm sure I attained a certain "religious literacy" in the fifth grade: I could list the ten commandments and the seven sacraments, and could even spell everything right. However, when I was a child the cognitive knowledge was of limited value. What is of much greater value remains, for me, the memory of my first catechist.

***TIME OUT!

Please think about what you have been reading, and consider these questions, either on your own or with another person:

1. Who was your "first catechist"?

2. What qualities did this person possess that helped you to learn about God, Church, or your own goodness?

3. Who is a catechist for you today? How does that person help you to learn about God, Church, and your own goodness?

Catechesis and Religious Literacy

Catechists, then, are clearly the most vital component in every experience of religious education or catechesis. Simply by *being* who they are and by living out their faith, catechists "teach" God to their students. But, as we continue to point out in this book, catechists are even more than people of faith: catechists are people of faith who can also articulate and express that faith in ways intended to lead students to knowledge and understanding of the faith tradition. Once understood, students then need to be able, like their catechists, to articulate and express what they have learned. This "religious literacy" is important if children today are to grow into adults who know what they're talking about in attempting to share both their personal faith as well as the faith tradition from which they have come.

Religious instruction that is based on educational or cognitive principles of learning can result in the religious literacy that is always a significant goal of all catechetical experiences. Contemporary programs of religious education must not, and do not, ignore the "what" of the faith tradition. The content of religious education is vital, but this content is present in many different ways. James Michael Lee has produced a lengthy but insightful trilogy concerned with theories of "religious instruction": *The Shape of Religious Instruction* (Dayton: Pflaum, 1971), *The Flow of Religious Instruction* (Dayton: Pflaum, 1973), and *The Content of Religious Instruction* (Birmingham: Religious Education Press, 1985). In these works, Lee notes some of the many ways in which "content" can be presented.

We come to an understanding of the faith tradition, says Lee in the third volume of the trilogy, *The Content of Religious Instruction*, by *experiencing* content. Content is found not only in the actual-factual material of the lesson, but also is present in all that surrounds it: the lifestyle of the catechist and the community of faith that gradually surrounds the learner in a non-verbal, affective, unconscious process of communicating faith. Lee states in the first volume of the trilogy, *The Shape of Religious Instruction,* that this process of assimilation of content is also brought about by deliberate, intentional, and consistent instruction. While Lee never denies the importance of life experience in forming faith, he seems to have moved beyond his earlier reliance on intentional instruction as the core method to a recognition of a more holistic view that includes the entire catechetical environment as being part of the content.

That was my experience as a child in a Catholic school classroom memorizing and reciting incomprehensible answers to obscure catechism questions. The environment taught me the meaning of those questions and answers. "Religious literacy" takes on new meaning when we consider just what it is we want children to be literate about. Do we merely want those we catechize to be "literate" in the sense that they can read and write about their religious heritage? Is it enough that they be well-informed, educated, and knowledgeable about what the religious tradition stands for? Or do we, as catechists, want more than that?

It seems to be fairly simple to "teach religion," to present the history, beliefs, and practices of a religious tradition. It is quite another thing to catechize, to "share faith" with another. In doing catechesis we put our own faith on the line by insisting that it matters to us. Our faith motivates us to take a stance, to really care about and live out the values of our religious tradition. We speak about the living God, alive in us and in those we catechize when we "do" catechesis. We are not impassive teachers; because we are passionate about what we have come to know about God we cannot merely present information. We instead speak of the ways God has been present to us and with us in the revelatory moments of our lives—in the persons, places, and events which have brought us to new awareness and insight into what God is like. We show by our attitudes and actions just what our response to God's love for us looks like—we attempt to be present to others as God is present to us, in loving service and care. We live our faith when we catechize, we don't just teach about it.

***TIME OUT!

As you stop to think about what you've been reading, please consider these questions, either on your own or with another person.

1. In the past year, what new insight have you gained about your lived faith that you *must* tell others about?

2. In the past year, what new knowledge about your faith tradition have you acquired that you now feel able to explain to others?

3. Where do you look for the "content" you bring to those you catechize?

Methodology and Religious Literacy

Religious literacy in the past was accomplished through didactic teaching methods, often not very concerned with the needs or the questions of the children. There was a curriculum based nearly exclusively on "The Teachings of the Church" rather than on the reality of life experience, and rarely did the two coincide. My old Baltimore Catechism contains an explanation of "sanctifying grace" that certainly does little to challenge the imagination of a normal intermediate-aged child: "Sanctifying grace makes us holy and pleasing to God. It makes us temples of the Holy Ghost. It gives us the right to heaven." The "principle ways of obtaining grace," it goes on to say, are "prayer and the sacraments, especially the Holy Eucharist." There is no further attempt to present the concept of grace in ways a child of nine or ten might understand, let alone relate to.

In contrast, the Grade Four text published by the Silver Burdett Ginn series *This Is Our Faith* (1991) defines grace as "God's gift of his own life and presence to people" and that "We believe that all God makes is good and shows God's goodness and love. God is always here with each one of us in our world. This is God's grace. It is God's gift to us. God's grace makes us like God." The lesson asks children to draw things that they "like a lot and think are very good." There is a poem about "All Good Things," and the creation story from Genesis 1–2:2 is presented with an opportunity for the children to write about "one of God's created gifts that especially interests you."

The contrast between these two ways of accomplishing some degree of religious literacy in children is profound. Today we attempt to legitimize the experiences of children and to help them to discover within those experiences how they might come to know God and to respond to what they are learning about God in reaching out to others. When we make connections between their life experiences and The Teachings of the Church (the Tradition) it is a double-whammy moment of truth.

We cannot deny what we have experienced (it rained today) and we cannot deny what that experience probably will mean to us (the spring flowers will begin to bloom soon). When we cannot deny the experience of forgiveness (my friend and I made up after a fight), we cannot deny what that experience probably means (if my friend forgives me, God does too). As catechists, it is possible, then, to make the connections with human experience, what Jesus had to say about the prodigal son's father, and even perhaps with "The Teachings of the Church" concerning the sacrament of penance.

Religious literacy, then, is accomplished through a multi-faceted methodology that combines educational theory, theology, psychology, spirituality, and sensitivity to life experience. Of course it is important that there be the ability to articulate in some fairly clear way to what degree religious literacy has been attained. Contemporary catechetical theory takes all of this into account, and the ways we approach religious literacy today reveal a dedication to this interdependent and interrelated system.

In this system, the usual grade-level catechetical programs focus on the developmental stages of the children in offering the most appropriate materials that will enhance their spiritual, psychological, and educational potential. Typical lessons contain components that recognize the importance of life experience, doctrinal content, and religious response, all developed according to the levels of understanding and capabilities of the child. And for many years now catechetical professionals have looked with gratitude upon these materials with the same reverence expressed during the process of creation: "God saw that it was good."

The development of catechetical theory and practice did not come to this level of quality overnight. Enormous strides have been made over the past years in the field of catechetics. From the indoctrination or doctrinal approach of the Baltimore Catechism to the kerygmatic or scriptural methodology of Joseph Jungmann and Johannes Hoffinger on through John Westerhoff's emphasis on socialization to Thomas Groome's shared praxis process and now (perhaps coming full circle?) with the arrival of *The Catechism of the Catholic Church,* we realize today that catechesis cannot remain static and immovable.

When I was growing up, the norm was to be static, immovable, and eternal. The Mass my family attended each Sunday was "said" in Latin, and I was taught that only this dead language was adequate to convey the unchanging teachings of the Church. I learned that God the Father created the world in seven days, Jesus died for my sins, and the Holy Spirit came on the day of my confirmation. In school we read Bible stories, never the Bible itself. We went to Mass every First Friday after which we ate our breakfasts brought from home. The kind Sisters presented an image of holiness and otherworldliness that I knew I could never attain. But they taught, I learned enough to please them and to earn good grades in religion, and when I left Catholic school I had little curiosity or interest in things religious. For all I knew it had all been covered for life, and the warranty was carefully filed away.

When I was older, and in need of repair, the ability to question, search, and discover had fortunately not deserted me. The experiences of life led me to ask those philosophical questions that, for those of us "trained" in a religious tradition, must lead to theological explorations. The "why's" of my existence (why am I who I am? why am I living at this time in this place? why do goodness and evil exist in my life?) demand answers. My religious tradition and my religious experience help me to move toward those answers.

Contemporary catechetical theory makes a clear distinction between the "teaching of religion," as I experienced it as a child, and catechesis, which has a broader perspective that involves searching and discovery. The ancient and venerable definition for "catechesis" has its roots in the concept of "re-echoing," of re-sounding what has been heard or handed on from an earlier source. Fr. Jim Dunning uses this language in the title of his excellent book about formation of catechists and homilists for teaching and preaching God's Word within the order of Christian initiation of adults: *Echoing God's Word* (Arlington, VA: The North American Forum on the Catechumenate, 1993). He defines that the Greek word "katechein" means "to sound down," a re-echoing down from one to another. Catechesis indeed echoes and re-echoes what has been discovered about God, from one generation to the next.

Catechisms, sharing the same etymology, are instructional summaries, often but certainly not always in question-and-answer form, that can be rather easily repeated or echoed. The process of handing on the faith through catechisms was popularized by Martin Luther after the invention of movable type and the proliferation of books. When a religious tradition is echoed or re-sounded from people to people and from age to age, its expression will vary according to the times, cultures, technological advances, and even ecclesial interpretation as doctrine is developed. But the basic source and focus of faith remains steady and constant: its communication will be modified according to changing patterns of expression and comprehension.

Thus the concept of echoing or re-sounding one's faith takes on a communal as well as a personal aspect. Within the community of faith we hand on what has been given to us. But it is only when we own the faith that results from what we have learned about our faith tradition as it connects with what we have experienced that we are able to share it with real authenticity. The faith community provides the environment, motivation, value system, and language that enables us to articulate what we have received. However, we find personal, unique, and individual ways to communicate to others the faith tradition that others, in their own personal and unique way, shared with us. In this way, God lives in us and through us, and we are "doing" catechesis.

Catechesis Defined

Catechesis today, then, is defined in many ways, all presenting a similar understanding. The definition from the General Catechetical Directory, #21, that was presented in Chapter One remains the most comprehensive: "Catechesis is the term to be used for that form of ecclesial action which leads both communities and individual members of the faithful to maturity of faith."

The National Catechetical Directory for Catholics of the United States, approved by the National Conference of Catholic Bishops in 1979, says in #32 much the same thing, but with embellishments:

> Catechesis is an esteemed term in Christian tradition. Its purpose is to make a person's faith become living, conscious, and active, through the light of instruction. . . . Catechesis is a lifelong process for the individual and a constant and concerted pastoral activity of the Christian Community.

Pope John Paul II goes a bit farther in his Apostolic Exhortation *Catechesi Tradendae (On Catechesis in Our Time),* 1979, as he makes these statements about catechesis:

> Authentic catechesis is always an orderly and systematic initiation into the revelation that God has given of himself to humanity in Christ Jesus, a revelation stored in the depths of the Church's memory and in Sacred Scripture, and constantly communicated from one generation to the next by a living, active "traditio." This revelation is not however isolated from life or artificially juxtaposed to it. It is concerned with the ultimate meaning of life and it illumines the whole of life with the light of the Gospel, to inspire it or to question it.

Catechesis as defined in these documents presents an image that is in contrast to the "teaching of religion" that I experienced. The teaching of religion and of religious practices and beliefs can be accomplished by anyone who has decent classroom management skills and who might be knowledgeable enough—or at least have access to teacher's guides—to do so. It is complicated, connected as it is to both content and context. There will be more about that later on in this book.

***TIME OUT!

But for now, please consider these questions. Think about them, write something if you wish, or discuss them with a friendly catechist of your choice.

Catechesis and the teaching of religion are not always the same. In looking at the following questions, do you see a difference in focus between "learning about the sacrament of penance" and being taught about God's mercy or punishment? If not, why not? If so, what makes the difference?

1. When you were growing up, how did you learn about the sacrament of penance?

2. Who taught you how to "go to confession"?

3. Who taught you about forgiveness?

4. Who taught you about God's mercy or punishment?

5. What methods were used?

6. How did you respond?

In my own reflection on these questions, I discover once again how thoroughly convinced I have become that while formal catechetical programs are extremely important, there is much more to catechesis than what goes on in structured and intentional learning sessions. This is, of course, not new or original insight, but in differentiating between those "who taught me how to go to confession" and those who taught me about mercy, forgiveness, and yes, even punishment, I see even more clearly how vitally necessary it is to keep an open-ended approach always in mind. If we have come to believe that there is indeed a process to catechesis, that knowing God is a lifelong endeavor, that we continuously grow in wisdom and understanding, and that an authentic faith response calls for ongoing, dynamic participation in this process, then we cannot settle for less than the best in our catechetical efforts.

As we end this section we can summarize by recognizing again the limitations of the memorization, indoctrination, and graded approach of my childhood. Certainly there are limitations to be found in catechetical approaches today as well, as Robert Duggan and Maureen Kelly so convincingly argue in *Christian Initiation of Children: Hope for the Future*. But as we have seen thus far in this book, progress continues to be made. Attempts to respect the anthropology that insists on the importance of human growth and development is a giant step in the right direction. Catechetical methodology such as Groome's Shared Christian Praxis also brings us closer to bridging the experiences of life and the experience of God. As John Westerhoff insists, religious communities such as parishes, schools, and families play perhaps the most vital role in socializing children to faith. Catechesis is both formal and informal, structured and unstructured. Both are important. Now, with the advent of lectionary-based catechesis, perhaps we can add another dimension to the ever-evolving process of catechesis.

If you'd like some further insight into these ideas, here are some resources:

Boys, Mary. *Educating in Faith*. San Francisco: Harper & Row, 1989.

Duggan, Robert, and Kelly, Maureen. *Christian Initiation of Children: Hope for the Future*. Mahwah, NJ: Paulist Press, 1991.

Groome, Thomas. *Sharing Faith*. New York: HarperCollins, 1991.

Lee, James Michael. *The Content of Religious Instruction*. Birmingham: Religious Education Press, 1985.

Lee, James Michael. *The Flow of Religious Instruction*. Dayton: Pflaum, 1973.

Lee, James Michael. *The Scope of Religious Instruction*. Dayton: Pflaum, 1971.

Warren, Michael, ed. *Sourcebook for Modern Catechetics*. Winona, MN: Saint Mary's Press, 1983.

Westerhoff, John, ed. *A Faithful Church*. Wilton, CN: Morehouse-Barlow, 1981.

4

Formation for Lectionary-Based Catechesis

A Catechist's Story

We have seen in previous chapters some ways in which an appreciation for the interconnectedness of catechesis, liturgy, and education affects the development of persuasive and useful catechetical theory and methodology. Effective lectionary-based catechesis demands that this mutuality be valued, respected, and honored. Each component of the triad is important if there is to be a genuine alliance among them. Lectionary-based catechesis will only come into its own as an authentic approach in bringing about maturity of faith when educational theory, catechesis, and liturgy come together. I like to think of these three components as the legs of a tripod, supporting the camera of faith through which it is possible to view and capture life. Through the lens of lectionary-based catechesis we just might possibly see more clearly what God is like and what God is calling us to be like.

However, one element is missing from this picture so far. The one who focuses the lens, the one who snaps the shutter, the one who determines the composition of the image is, of course, the catechist. If lectionary-based catechesis is to be anything more than the latest "CCD" gimmick, if lectionary-based catechesis can indeed be part of the "ecclesial action" that can lead people and communities to maturity of faith, if lectionary-based catechesis is, as the kids say, "for real," then it is the catechist who is ultimately responsible for making it happen.

However, catechists are formed, not born, and the story of my own journey as a catechist is perhaps the best way to illustrate this notion. I consider myself to be a good and effective catechist, but certainly a much better and more effective catechist now than when I started. When I was a young mother, it was my chosen role to stay home with the children and to bake the allegorical cookies of which Hillary Rodham Clinton once spoke. My husband went off to work each day, slaying the dragons of the corporate world to provide the necessities of life for us. After the birth of our fourth child, I was eager to escape the tedium of domestic responsibility and volunteered to teach a parish CCD class on Sunday mornings when Dad was home, allowing me the freedom to dash off without trundling three or four little people with me. For some unknown reason I seemed to think that spending a few hours each week with other people's children would be more interesting and fascinating than being with my own. I also believed that I had no particularly spectacular talents to volunteer other than the ability to relate to children, being quite thoroughly experienced in that field.

I had taught my own children their prayers. I had talked to them about God from time to time as we marveled at God's wonderful creation on walks and in examining the newest baby's tiny toes. I lectured them about fairness and honesty and tried to model those values as much as humanly possible when confronted with sibling rivalry and the frequent arbitration of insignificant and ridiculous issues. I read "holy" books to them such as the Little Golden Books about creation, the birthday of Baby Jesus, and David and Goliath. Their father and I took them with us to Mass every Sunday and holy day and even to confession on a regular basis, we attended PTA meetings at the parish school which the older ones attended, and we always prayed, holding hands, before meals. I thought this background was all that was necessary to teach CCD to fourth graders. Not!

I discovered very early on just how difficult it was to speak with any real conviction about my Catholic faith. I did not have the language to articulate to children what little I really knew about what I thought I knew about God, church, Jesus. The curriculum for the fourth grade at that time was centered around the ten commandments, which I originally thought would be a snap. Easy to teach children not to kill or even not to punch each other out, not to steal, not to swear or tell lies, right? Wrong! I found that lecturing them was totally ineffective and that I would have to come up with something a little more engrossing. Furthermore, that sixth commandment was awfully hard to explain to nine-year-olds. I struggled a lot that first year, and only the delight I took in the children and the occasional moments of pure inspiration got me through.

What was more important, however, was that I discovered a lot about myself, as a Christian woman attempting to express my understandings of who/what/where God was for me in my life. I attended a catechist formation course (they called it "teacher training" then) that winter, and soon I was off and running. I was absolutely transfixed, awed, by the new ideas I heard. I devoured all the handouts, asked countless questions, began to beg, borrow, and even buy quasi-theological books. It was as if the faith questions of my childhood, locked up and inaccessible within the Baltimore Catechism of my school days and in the obscure traditions of my early years, suddenly were released in a surge of searching, discovering, and pursuit of knowledge. I really became rather obnoxious in my zeal to learn and to express what I was coming to know.

In all of this excitement over what I was learning, however, I was somehow led to a deeper and more profound awareness of God in my life. I was surprised to discover myself praying often, in what quiet times I could find within the insanity of family activities. My spiritual life grew along with my theological and catechetical curiosity. Mass and eucharist became meaningful to me in ways I had never before experienced as I moved through an intellectual into a spiritual conversion.

In the midst of all of this, I actually did begin to make some progress in that Sunday morning CCD class with the fourth graders. I found that it was easier to speak of God to them now that I had a somewhat better idea of who/what/where God was in my life, for me. I found a language that had meaning for me, and I could now begin to translate my language into language that had meaning for nine-year-olds. I learned that I could speak about "sacrament" or "grace" or "eucharist" out of my own earned understanding, my own experience. I was no longer merely presenting the content of the children's religion text: I was presenting the content of my own faith. The paradox of faith development, however, is that each new insight leads to new questions which in turn lead to a faith response that demands further insight. And so my formation as a catechist continues, in a circular and unending spiral, to this day.

***TIME OUT!

Again you are asked to reflect about what you have been reading. Please take a few minutes to consider the following questions either alone or with another catechist:

1. When did you first become involved in religious education? Who invited you?

2. What was your initial response to the "invitation"? What is your response now? Would you do it again?

3. Describe one of your successful catechetical experiences, either as a catechist or as a learner. What made this a good experience?

4. Describe one of your less pleasant catechetical experiences, either as a catechist or as a learner. What would you change if you were to do it over?

Formation and Process: A Necessary Combination

Catechists who are formed, not born, will readily admit that certain knowledge and skills are necessary if they are to be agents of effective catechesis. But the knowledge and skills are useless if there is not present in the catechist the awareness of God's presence within and among the ordinary things that make up daily living. The real test of an effective and faith-filled catechist is in his or her ability to make and then to express those connections between one's experience of God and of church and one's experience of life.

This doesn't just happen: it is a life-long and ongoing process demanding awareness and response that cannot be boxed up, once and for all. Catechist formation is a continuing process just as is all formation in faith, and catechist formation for doing lectionary-based catechesis is no exception. At the same time, it is recognized that catechists who can effectively integrate the Sunday lectionary readings into their catechetical sessions will perhaps require a special and somewhat different type of formation than the more traditional formation programs have offered to catechists in the past.

The effective formation of lectionary-based catechists relies greatly on the concept of "process," just as effective lectionary-based catechesis requires a sense of ongoingness in its methodology. In lectionary-based catechesis the nature of an ongoing format throughout the three year liturgical cycle contributes to the formation process of those being catechized. So too with the formation of catechists who begin to view the lectionary as an integral part of their own formation in faith.

Process, we know, must be endured patiently. If we could just leap into final and complete maturity at a given age we wouldn't have to undergo the growing pains required by process. Americans are considered "mature" enough to marry without parental consent and to vote at age 18, to drink intelligently at age 21, and to retire from work at age 65. It would be lovely if we could program our spiritual, emotional, and psychological maturity in such a way, but of course it just doesn't work like that. If we are truly honest in our assessments of our own abilities to grow and develop, we accept process as a necessary aspect of the continuum toward maturity.

Process is experienced in various ways. In our contemporary world of immediate access to everything, the idea of process can be almost incomprehensible for those reared in a Mac-Instant milieu. Once upon a time I baked the best chocolate chip cookies on the block; now, Mrs. Fields does that for me, instantly. My mother's slow-cooked standing rib roasts were an incredible treat, especially the left-overs shredded into sandwiches. Now it's stop at Arby's for roast beef in a flash. Books take time to read and reread when the language is delicious and evocative and you can't *bear* for the book to end. The same stories can be told in a 118-minute video, and then sometimes you can't *wait* for them to end.

My children grew slowly, slowly through their very young years while I waited impatiently for them to crawl, walk, feed themselves, run, speak in words and finally in sentences. And suddenly, instantly, they have become adults with a stubborn autonomy that seems to have no relationship to those dependent little people. Process is responsible for and an inevitable part of our existence even in our desire to disregard it.

Like the slow and gentle awakening of love for another person, process occurs as knowledge and understanding increase. Process cannot be hurried; the accumulation of wisdom and insight is often so gradual that we can be almost unaware of changes in outlook or perspective. The process of loving, for instance, moves from initial encounter through fascination with the other to a need to communicate deeply and then continues onward to eventual commitment and ultimate concern for the other's welfare more than our own. All of this takes time, measured in human or psychological terms. Process happens when we take time out to consider, to reflect, to ponder, and when we ask a lot of "why?" questions.

The cyclical nature of process is time-dependent, with season following season, everything at its own pace, in its own time. Insights emerge, recede, and re-emerge with increasing clarity. Doubts surface, are confronted more or less satisfactorily, and are put aside for a while. Eventually this process/cycle can lead to a conscious awareness of growth having taken place, that we have indeed discovered something new about ourselves, our world, and our God. And then we begin all over again.

***TIME OUT!

Does what you've been reading make sense to you? Please think about your own process of maturation as you consider these questions, either on your own or with another person.

1. Which words best describe your approach toward moving along in your own maturation process: "reliable and consistent" or "spontaneous and unpredictable"?

2. What in your own life would you have liked to hurry along? to slow down?

3. What in your life is worth waiting for? is not worth waiting for?

Catechists who will be doing lectionary-based catechesis recognize the value of respecting this cyclical aspect of process, both in their own faith life and in the faith life of those they catechize as well. Catechists know that wisdom and understanding do not emerge full-blown, once and for all, never to be considered again. They "teach and review, teach and review," relatively content with the idea that their message will be heard differently each time according to the current level of awareness and need of those they catechize. The cyclical nature of process is recognized as one of the important components, too, in the design and experience of liturgical celebration.

There is something inherently natural about the process of cyclical worship. To gather on a regular basis as a faith community seems to be a comfortable and right thing to do for most of us. Perhaps this tendency comes out of the socialization or even conditioning process we experienced during our Catholic Wonder Years. Nonetheless, if in our maturation journey we progressed in a relatively normal way through some of the various stages of faith development, we probably undertook the task of healthy rebellion and resistance at some point in our adult years and turned away, either physically or with internal revolt, from the prescribed Sunday Mass.

If the liturgical experience of our childhood had been reasonably expressive of our faith values it is likely that as we continued our passage through life we "returned"—either physically or from our internal resistance—to Mass on a regular basis. We began to appropriate a faith of our own, to take ownership of the faith we inherited from our families, because we recognized in those faith values something constitutive of our deepest needs and yearnings for the God we were beginning to know.

As adults we have come to realize the significance of a cycle of worship that occurs weekly, or even daily. In spite of our perhaps instinctive resistance to the old mandate that required attendance at Sunday Mass "under the pain of mortal sin," this idea should not be totally rejected in this contemporary period of liturgical enlightenment. There are times for all of us when going to Mass seems like the last thing we want to do on a Sunday morning, but because of a sense of the rightness of it, and maybe just because after all it *is* Sunday, we go. Of course it is always hoped that Sunday liturgy will be done prayerfully and well and that people will choose to be there rather than at the mall or at the beach or simply sleeping in with the Sunday papers. People will choose the Sunday Mass because at Mass they are able to experience a true and authentic encounter with God, to say nothing of their desire to be a part of the parish faith community with whom there is a sense of familial social and spiritual comfort.

At the same time, however, we know from present social science research (as well as from ancient philosophers and Christian mystics) that we human beings seem to thrive when there is a sense of order in our lives. When a predictable way of doing things exists, when people know fairly well what to expect, we "hold on" to previously learned knowledge and move forward in our lives in a healthy way. When good, meaningful, and prayerful liturgical celebration is a consistent event that occurs regularly, there is that sense of moving forward through the years with an ever-changing, ever-new realization of God's presence in our world.

The lectionary readings do much to contribute to a sense of process. By its very nature the lectionary is a vital part of the process of liturgical celebration, helping to provide this consistency as the Sunday readings repeat, recycle, and revive our appreciation for the stories of faith that we hear over and over, always with new understandings as we continue to grow and change throughout our lives.

It could be interesting to chart via diary or journal the unfolding insight into our own (and our communal) spiritual, theological, and even psychological growth that might be occurring throughout a number of lectionary cycles or years. For instance, in reading from our journal of three or six years ago we could certainly be enlightened by our responses at that time to the obscure meaning of Matthew 20:1–16, the "unjust" landowner who pays workers hired late in the day the same wages as those who labored in the heat and sun for the entire day. It is quite possible that as that gospel passage recurs this year we might indeed have grown in our understandings of what it means to consider God's mysterious mercy as we again ponder the significance of the final phrase from that reading: "Thus the last shall be first and the first shall be last." And we might even be motivated to take that new insight with us as we reconsider ways in which we ourselves could live out God's mysterious justice and mercy in our everyday lives as employers, workers, and laborers of all kinds.

Scripture as a Vital Part of Formation

Catechists who are convinced that the Sunday readings have considerable value and that the Sunday readings can and do contribute to a deepening of faith recognize the foundational importance of scripture in their own lives. Scripture, for them, is a source of comfort and challenge, truth and mystery, knowledge and questioning. Catechists who are grounded in praying, studying, and responding to scripture realize that this is not just an "only on Sunday" way of life. The Bible becomes a frequent and delightful companion that accompanies their days.

But this familiarity with sacred scripture does not come easily, particularly for Catholics. Some of us who are old enough to remember a Bible-free Catholic education were told from an early age that the Bible was not for us to read. Instead, we read *about* the Bible through the medium of Bible Stories that glorified The First Sin of Adam and Eve or that presented a radiantly sentimentalized version of when The Angel Gabriel Appears to Mary. We learned that we were not "worthy" to understand the mysterious content of the real Bible. Nor were ordinary priests or nuns considered knowledgeable in biblical interpretation. Even seminary curricula did not contain courses in scripture. Catholic scripture scholars might have been included among the ranks of those qualified to read and interpret the Bible, but we did not know of the existence of such scholars because at that time in the world of popular Catholic culture they were hidden from view like faintly embarrassing black-sheep relatives. Many Protestants, on the other hand, could and did read the Bible. Modern scripture scholarship has its roots in Protestant biblical study and interpretation. But for Catholics, this Protestant emphasis on the Bible somehow excluded Protestants from the ranks of Catholic holiness and sacramental life. It was thought that Catholics had more to offer the faithful than just "the Bible," and so it was not necessary for Catholics to know anything about the Bible. It was not until Pius XII issued his encyclical *Divino Afflante Spiritu* in 1943 that Catholic biblical scholarship was even officially permitted, and Catholics have been catching up ever since.

After Vatican II when people began to actually read the scriptures, it seemed that the Bible suddenly became Catholic. It was with great excitement that we discovered the beauty of biblical language and the profound wisdom to be found in scripture. Creation, covenant, and commandments led to sin, prophetic warnings, and final restoration. Jesus, once he arrived on the scene, became *real* to me as I read and reread stories of his compassion, forgiveness, and selfless love. Catholics everywhere flocked to Bible-study groups, as I did. We had a wonderful time, freed at last from our childhood inhibitions as we were allowed to voice uninformed questions and to state our naive opinions about what this or that passage might possibly mean to us here and now.

Young catechists today are fortunate in having grown up with the Bible that became Catholic. They have no history of a reluctance to read and interpret sacred scripture. They were taught as children how to find chapter and verse. They know the mutuality that exists between sacred scripture and the sacramental life of the Church because they have experienced both. But there is still a good deal that could be done to enable the formation of scripturally-sensitive catechists who are concerned about including and presenting scripture in a substantive and essential way.

When Sunday readings form the backbone of catechetical sessions for children, the catechists who direct these sessions must be comfortable with their own understandings of those readings. The language of scripture must come easily to them. They need to be able to use "God talk" without embarrassment. The words and actions of the catechists' prayer reveal a very personal faith, and this cannot be phony or unreal. In short, catechists who speak of the God of scripture speak of the God of their own experience and understanding as well.

A comparison can be made between the "comfort zones" that must be inhabited by those who present scripture-based catechesis and by those involved in sexuality education. In both cases the ideas and concepts need to be offered with genuine integrity and authority. Teachers in sexuality education programs who are at ease with their own sexuality, for instance, will have little difficulty using accurate language for body parts, offering graphic descriptions and illustrations of sexual activity, or responding to questions with clarity and openness. It is important that those doing sexuality education possess a certain ability to be matter-of-fact, objective, and non-judgmental. And yet their own values are almost certain to emerge, especially when this material is presented within the context of a moral tradition based on religious faith. An emphasis on commitment, fidelity, and unity will be part of how sexuality not only is taught but also is lived out by those whose perspective is grounded in a faith-filled response to those religious beliefs. Teachers who accept these virtues will see them as part of the whole learning experience and will use a methodology that refers back again and again to these themes.

So it is with catechists who are grounded in the values of scripture-based catechesis. They too will return again and again to scriptural themes as they catechize. They too will inhabit a kind of "comfort zone" when they speak of God; they will be at ease with their willingness to express and articulate their own experiences of God. Their vocabulary will be accurate, using the language of scripture and of their own personal faith in a matter-of-fact way, neither sentimentalizing its message nor resorting to melodramatic interpretations to make a point. Catechists will appreciate and appropriate the many images of God that scripture reveals and that they have come to understand, and they will not be locked into a particular image that limits the emergence and growth of authentic and mature faith.

***TIME OUT!

Once again you are invited to think about what you have been reading as you consider the following questions, either on your own or in discussion with another person.

1. At what age did you first begin to read the Bible? In what context did this happen: school, home, church, with friends, a Bible study or educational setting?

2. Do you see any parallels between sexuality education and scripture-based catechesis? If so, what are they?

3. What is your "comfort level" in speaking about your personal relationship with God? Please rank on a scale of 1 to 5 according to this scale and use your discoveries for further insight and understanding.

1 = very uncomfortable: embarrassed, feel my privacy is being invaded, cannot verbalize spontaneous prayer in front of others but join in group prayer and song.

2 = somewhat uncomfortable: sometimes stumble over "God" words, resort to traditional titles and language, difficulty praying spontaneously with others but I try.

3 = neutral comfort zone: use storytelling to illustrate my relationship with God, more comfortable speaking of God in the abstract, can pray aloud with others only when I have prepared what I will say.

4 = comfortable: easy to use personal examples of God in my life, spontaneous prayer with others is a meaningful communication with God, God is real to me and therefore comfortable to talk about.

5 = *very comfortable:* use many images and titles in speaking of God and in spontaneous prayer with others, God-talk occurs naturally in ordinary conversation, can voice doubts and questions about the mystery of God in my life and in the life of my faith community.

A Catechist Formation Program Based on Scriptural Formation

As catechists become more comfortable with God-talk and with scripture, they can begin to move into an appreciation of the process of lectionary-based catechesis with relative ease. Catechists who have discovered the value of scripture in their own study, prayer, and response to God's call find a deeper awareness of the importance of scripture as it is encountered in the liturgical setting. The lectionary readings offer a week-by-week account of God's action in the lives of people of faith, a sort of scriptural soap opera minus the commercials. Catechists as well as those they catechize hear these wonderful stories as the word of God is proclaimed within the environment of the liturgical setting. The catechist can take advantage of this mutual experience when moving into lectionary-based catechesis. The story of salvation becomes real as catechists do what catechists do best: make connections between the "then" of the lectionary readings and the "now" of everyday life. It is a natural process for catechists who are scripturally sensitive to move from a somewhat distanced scripture-based catechesis into a more comprehensive approach based on lectionary readings. Lectionary-based catechesis continues what scripture-based catechesis has begun.

We know, then, that sacred scripture has the capacity to be a vital component in the continuing formation of catechists and in their ability to catechize well when scripture has been a vital part of their faith experience. However, it is also true that in preparing catechists for lectionary-based catecheis it is important to realize that some catechists have not been grounded in scripture throughout their lives and many are just awakening to the challenge and potential for spiritual growth that a study of scripture offers to them. When examining some possibilities for the preparation of more scripturally sensitive catechists who will move smoothly into lectionary-based catechesis it is important to take into consideration both the strengths and the limitations of the formative process and when necessary attempt to fill in around the edges in the best possible ways.

In designing a program of formation for catechists who will be involved in lectionary-based catechesis, it would be good to consider some basic skills and knowledge that they would need before they could move forward in further growth. This is not to say that an intellectual "knowledge" of scripture is the primary need of catechists or of anyone else other than perhaps scripture scholars engaged in technical or primarily theological investigations.

This is also not to say that such "knowledge" is of no importance. Quite to the contrary: a basic familiarity with any topic is of course essential if one is to be capable of eliciting the belief of others. In catechesis, "knowledge" results not only from what has been experienced but also from what has been discovered or learned. Knowledge of the Bible is a "both–and" situation: both cognitive learning and spiritual awareness of God in the lives of believers lead to what is "known" about the scriptural tradition. Therefore, it is important to be confident that the catechist possesses to a certain degree the foundational information about the Bible before moving on to matters of exegesis, personal interpretation, and prayerful response.

The first step in such a program of catechist formation, then, would be to begin with the basics. There are some questions that could be asked of catechists, a kind of "pre-catechesis" needs assessment or inventory that could be helpful in determining where to begin in preparing catechists for lectionary-based catechesis.

It is recommended that the parish catechetical leader meet with catechists to discuss this "inventory" with them, either in very small groups (no more than four) or individually. It is hoped that a friendly and congenial relationship exists among the catechists and the catechetical leader, and that in no way would the catechetical leader suggest that this is a "test." Needs inventories are certainly not tests, but rather are intended to accomplish exactly what their name implies: merely to determine needs of the learners so that appropriate programs can be designed that will meet those needs.

Pre-Catechesis Inventory

In an informal, comfortable, and hospitable environment (don't forget the coffee, tea, or soft drinks!), the catechetical leader can discuss with the catechists the following issues related to the catechists' current understanding of scripture.

1. How scripturally literate is the catechist? Does the catechist have the necessary knowledge and skills to:
— locate chapter and verse?

— understand the relationship and divisions between the Old Testament and the New Testament?

— name the gospel writers?

— find in the Bible some key themes in both OT and NT such as creation, covenant, prophecy, some of the major teachings of Jesus, death, resurrection?

— know about and locate the Acts of the Apostles, the letters of Paul and the other pastoral letters, the book of Revelation?

2. How does the catechist experience scripture at this point in his or her life? Ask:

— What part does scripture play in your everyday life?

— How do you currently make use of scripture? in study? in prayer? in times of crisis or joy? daily or weekly or occasionally according to need and motivation?

3. What does the catechist want to know about the Bible? What questions does the catechist have? What has provoked curiosity or interest? Ask the catechist:

— If you were asked to explain to a person of another religious tradition what the Bible was, just how would you phrase your definition of the word "Bible"?

— Why would you want to read the Bible?

— What puzzles you most about the Bible?

— What is your favorite or most familiar Bible passage or story?

The outcome of this interview between catechetical leader and catechists can certainly result in the design of a formation program that more fully "fills in" around the edges of the catechists' experience of sacred scripture. The catechetical leader can also determine at this time how literally the catechists are approaching scripture and to what extent the formation program will need to deal with a fundamentalist approach on the part of the catechists. The interview can also have the added advantage of building relationships and establishing a basis for future encounters as the catechists move into a more structured formation program that will prepare them for doing lectionary-based catechesis. Catechist formation programs, for biblical formation or whatever other specific purpose they might be designed, are necessary for many, many reasons, not the least of which is the opportunity for spiritual growth such as I began to experience in my first catechist formation program years ago. But there are other rationales for catechist formation as well, and some basic principles to keep in mind.

Basic Principles of Catechist Formation

The first and foremost consideration for all those who are involved in leading or facilitating educational endeavors is of course to be aware of the needs of the learners. In catechesis this is even more true. Catechists have needs, concerns, expectations that must be met if they are to grow in the faith that they will share with others. The needs of catechists are, in many ways, the needs we all have: to care and to be cared for, to be taken seriously, to be affirmed, to be part of a good and worthwhile group, to know what we're talking about and to be offered opportunities for further growth in knowledge and wisdom.

Adult learners have different needs than do immature learners. Adults, or mature learners, take responsibility for their own learning: it is not the primary responsibility of the "teacher" that learning occurs. Leon McKenzie states in *The Religious Education of Adults* (Birmingham: Religious Education Press, 1982, p. 129): "It is agreed that adults are more self-directing than children, that adults have had more experiences than children, that adults are more independent than children, that adult readiness to learn is related to concerns arising from their life situations, and that adults seek to apply what they learn as soon as possible . . ." In the teaching of adults, then, the one who is engaged in presenting information facilitates and enables the learning process to occur, but it is the adult learners who take responsibility for what they actually do, in fact, choose to learn.

Adults can participate in the design of their own learning agenda, knowing that they will pursue a course of discovery that answers the questions they have. While there are certainly objective standards to be met in programs of adult education, the content of these programs must take seriously what it is adults want to know. Adults resist a curriculum that provides answers to questions that have not yet been asked, and they can be stubbornly antagonistic to anyone attempting to teach them something they have no interest or motivation in learning.

I have had several experiences, much to my distress and to theirs, when I forgot how important it is to respect the autonomy of adult learners. Once, many years ago when I was coordinating adult religious education activities in my parish, the pastor decided that the parishioners needed to know more about changes in the Mass that were going on after the close of the Second Vatican Council. This was certainly an admirable intention on his part, since it seemed that every week at Mass something new was added, like English, or deleted, like altar rails or Latin. He requested that I "do something" to teach folks about what was going on.

I dutifully obtained a set of filmstrips (remember them?) from the diocesan office of religious education and advertised a Sunday-morning-after-Mass adult education program. Exactly one person came. Apparently parishioners had not yet formulated enough questions about liturgical changes to seek answers. Until they did (and they did, when we tried again a year or so later when they had become thoroughly confused and uncertain and even angry), all such efforts were in vain. Adults—mature learners—choose what, when, and how to learn.

The faith life of adults has been studied by James Fowler and others, as we noted earlier, and it has been verified that adult faith does not "increase" because of knowledge. It appears to be the other way around: knowledge increases because of faith. One of the most obvious indicators of mature faith is a religious curiosity which allows for searchings, doubt, and questions. Mature faith arises from the desire to discover for oneself what God is like, and this does not happen until those questions are allowed to surface. It is the wonderful opportunity for those involved in the faith formation of adults to encourage the questions and therefore to aid in the discovery of a faith that is truly owned.

James Fowler has done considerable research and writing about stages of faith, and in *Becoming Adult, Becoming Christian* (San Francisco: Harper and Row, 1984, p. 75) he defines "faith" as "a way of being and moving" in this world in order to make sense of our lives and to move "from the limiting love of those who love us and on whom we are dependent, toward the limitless love that comes from genuine identification with the Source and Center of all being." This means searching, growing, changing. As Fowler puts it on p. 142: "Perspectives on adult development alert us to the fact that . . . we will be testing, shaping, and re-forming the ways we relate to others and the world, as well as revising the ways in which we image ourselves. When we consider the dynamics of faith in our lives, we sense that at each of the crisis points of our lives and at each of the expected or unexpected turning points of our lives, we face a time when our ways of making meaning and the patterns of our trusts and loyalties are subject to testing and change. We are getting used to the idea that adulthood is not static. We are coming to terms with the insight that change is normative, continuous, and consequential."

In these programs of adult catechesis, then, there are no tests, no grades, no evaluations of knowledge. Ideally, the issue of accountability should be considered within the context of faith growth, but since this is not measurable in quite the same the way that cognitive knowledge can be measured, a certain relaxing of the need for accountability on the part of the learner must be expected.

Another significant learning principle, however, is the one asserting that something has not been learned until it can be expressed in some way. It is possible to appropriate this concept in the catechesis of adults by encouraging them to keep journals, to write reflection papers, or to record on tape what it is they are coming to understand about their God, their religious tradition, and their faith. Another way to express what one has come to know is to witness, to tell others. Faith sharing, whether organized within the format of the catechist formation program or in informal settings over coffee or on the telephone, can enable this expression of what is being learned. Stanley Hauerwas, in his article "On Witnessing Our Story" in *Schooling Christians* (Stanley Hauerwas and John Westerhoff, eds., Grand Rapids: Eerdmans Publishing Company, 1992, p. 231), makes the point clearly: "The only way we can educate is through witness. What we must understand is that witness is necessary because we are so storied."

Self-evaluations are also very helpful for adults who are trying to go beyond the learning environment of their childhood which included so many exams, so many grades. One of the goals of adult catechesis should be to assist them in every way possible to continue to search out whatever it takes for them to come more completely to the fullness and deepening of faith.

In programs of catechist formation, then, some of these principles of adult learning should be taken into consideration: (1) adults take responsibility for their own learning, (2) adults will seek answers to their own questions, (3) adults are capable of self-evaluation and accountability, (4) adults can and will express what they have learned, and (5) adults are in process.

We have already spoken about process, and the need for gradual and ongoing faith formation. Catechists are in process, as we all are as we travel our journeys of faith. New experiences, new challenges, new understandings, and new opportunities to care for and to be cared for landmark our travels. Each is a step leading inevitably to the next, and in time we reach certain goals along the way. An appreciation of process is absolutely necessary in catechist formation. It is essential in a catechist formation program that adequate time is allowed for reflection and response.

In a practical sense, then, this means that formation as process should not be accomplished in haste in an attempt to get it all into a 30-hour course over the period of a week. I once completed a 3-unit course (a total of 45 classroom hours) in two weeks. The class was held from 8:00 a.m. to 12:30 each day for ten days. This was basically a course designed to achieve cognitive learning: it focused on historical and contemporary approaches to and theories of religious education. I was very motivated to learn because this topic was one I needed to know so that it could be included in courses I would be teaching myself one day. I taped the lectures and took voluminous notes. I discussed with others in the class at breaks and over lunch, read the required texts, and in short *lived* that class for the entire two weeks. Of course I have forgotten some of what I once thought I knew, retaining only those parts that I have continued to use in my teaching. I often wish that there had been more time to assimilate the material and perhaps more importantly to have had time to reflect on and make connections between what I was learning and my own faith life. Instead, it was information rather than formation that became the focus of my efforts. The schedule I experienced is probably not recommended in programs of catechist *formation!*

A catechist *formation* program, especially one designed to meet the needs of those preparing for lectionary-based catechesis, means exactly that: formation is the operative word. It can be argued that a 30-hour course presented six hours a day for five days can result in lots of information but probably little formation. When information is desired, this is more than likely not so bad a way to proceed. But what would a possible time frame look like that allows adequate formation in faith to occur? What is "enough" time for this to happen? We spend a lifetime, whatever our span of days might be, trying to come to faith. How, then, can we possibly design a program of formation that allows for the necessary time? To answer that question, at least from an admittedly subjective point of view, let's think again of the human cycles of time we spoke about earlier.

If weekly cycles of worship seem to be fairly natural to us, could we not accept weekly cycles of formation to be just as natural? Even the wonderful creation stories in Genesis rely on a seven-day cycle to make a point: there seems to be something "right" about that number seven! Perhaps it seems "right" for catechists to come together once a week to pray, study, and participate in their formation process.

Catechists who are to be concerned with lectionary-based catechesis have their own formational needs and expectations. Emphasis on scripture and liturgy is vital. Weekly sessions seem appropriate and it is natural to expect that the Sunday readings will be the basis for catechesis in these sessions. Principles of adult learning must, of course, be in place. At the same time, a methodology that can be used with children should emerge from the adult formation process. Effective lectionary-based catechesis for children begins with effective lectionary-based catechists.

What would a program of formation for catechists who are concerned with lectionary-based catechesis look like if some of these concepts were in place? A suggested course outline that might be used by parish or diocesan catechetical leaders in the formation of lectionary-based catechists can be found in the Appendix of this book. This outline is based roughly on the original Master Catechist program developed in the late 1970's and early 1980's by Fr. David Sork and the Office of Religious Education for the Archdiocese of Los Angeles. My experience as a member of the advisory board for that program has been one of the catechetical highlights of my life and I continue to value what I learned all those years ago. The course outline presented in the Appendix is an adaptation adjusted to meet the needs of catechists preparing to do lectionary-based catechesis.

Catechists who are indeed formed well and who are motivated to take their formation seriously will move into new and creative ways of doing catechesis, such as integrating lectionary readings and curriculum-based materials. Now we need to take a look at a method for these innovative catechists that can be used in putting it all together. But in the meantime, here are some more resources to consider.

Cully, Iris, and Cully, Kendig Brubaker, eds. *Harper's Encyclopedia of Religious Education*. San Francisco: Harper & Row, 1990.

Fowler, James W. *Becoming Adult, Becoming Christian*. San Francisco: Harper & Row, 1984.

Fowler, James W. *Stages of Faith*. San Francisco: Harper & Row, 1981.

Hauerwas, Stanley, and Westerhoff, John, eds. *Schooling Christians: "Holy Experiments" in American Education*. Grand Rapids, MI: Wm. B. Eerdmans Publishing, 1992.

Hill, Brennan R. *Key Dimensions of Religious Education*. Winona, MN: Saint Mary's Press, 1988.

McKenzie, Leon. *The Religious Education of Adults*. Birmingham: Religious Education Press, 1982.

Sork, David A., Boyd, Don, and Sedano, Maruja. *The Catechist Formation Book*. New York: Paulist Press, 1981.

Stokes, Kenneth, ed. *Faith Development in the Adult Life Cycle*. New York: W. H. Sadlier, 1982.

5

Putting It All Together: A Method for Catechists

Curriculum-Based Education

In previous chapters we have looked at some of the reasons for considering the adoption of a lectionary-based catechetical approach in parish programs of religious education. We have examined the history and rationale for this approach and have discovered some of the ways catechists can be formed and prepared for the effective use of lectionary-based catechesis in handing on the faith to children. We have reviewed some scriptural and liturgical principles which are necessary for the development and presentation of an effective lectionary-based catechesis. In addition, we have taken a brief look at some of the educational and catechetical principles that apply in suggesting a lectionary-based approach.

We have also seen in previous chapters how catechesis has been experienced in the past, for better for worse. We have done a bit of reminiscing, recalling how it was to "grow up Catholic" and to be socialized into a religious tradition. We have remembered early attempts to learn and to teach "the truths of our faith," and the memories of both experiences seem to fill us with a strange mixture of embarrassment and pride.

The current catechetical situation finds us in a world of transition. We seem to be somewhere in between the curriculum-based, cognitive programs of religious education that admittedly are a great improvement over the Baltimore Catechism but which still lack a certain ability to connect with the life of the parish community, and lectionary-based catechesis that connects well with the life of the parish community but is rather unclear in its content and methodology. As in all periods of transition, it is important to look clearly at not only what is possible in the future but also at what *was* possible in the past. Certainly many of the valuable aspects of curriculum-based programs of religious education will be retained even as they are retooled into new forms.

In the world of curriculum-based programs, there are many advantages and opportunities. This is a world of the well-educated, thinking Catholic who probably attended Catholic elementary and secondary schools and might even have graduated from Notre Dame University or Boston College. In the religious education of this person, the movement from the more simple theological concepts to the more complex has been gradual and always suited to whatever learning capabilities were present at each stage of development. Beginning concepts of God emerge from the Pre-K, K, and Grade One curriculum: God is Creator, Father, and one who loves us, "his" creatures. In later primary years, God is presented in the person of Jesus. God is further revealed in the intermediate and adolescent years in the moral code, sacramental experiences, and traditions of the Catholic Church. Often, as this inhabitant of the world of cognitive learning based on a course of studies reaches adulthood and an assumed level of maturity, the understanding of "God" becomes a question—and then only if and when the answers that were provided during childhood no longer sufficiently match the questions of an adult faith.

Learning skills, in a person grounded in a curriculum-based catechetical program, are focused on the three R's of religious literacy: reading, writing, and reasoning. The student is expected to be capable of comprehending written information (text books, reference materials, printed resources), of expressing in writing what has been taught (tests, research papers, "fill-in-the-blank" activities), and of arriving at logical conclusions based on reasonable data (learning basic principles and formulas, discussions, problem-solving activities). Thinking skills and language proficiency play a large part in curriculum-based catechetical programs.

In this curriculum-based world, the tried and the true is the norm. There is an historical precedence that gives new meaning to the motto "We've always done it this way." Many Roman Catholic religious traditions and practices reflect the world view of centuries of Western European civilization that had its origin in a Greco-Roman philosophical milieu that promoted rational thinking and logical reasoning. This implies an "education" model as part of those traditions and practices: a classroom environment, directed by one who teaches the prescribed content to students who are expected to achieve the learning objectives laid out for them by the educator. This traditional and historically successful method of educating children for proficiency in knowledge of secular topics has been appropriated in educating children for proficiency in knowledge of doctrine and Church teaching. In both cases there is an expectation that children will learn and will apply what they have learned to their life situations as they grow and mature.

In this educational setting, learning is valued not only for its own sake but also for how knowledge can be translated into employment opportunities and some degree of material success. The measurement of a person's worth is often connected with earning power that is possible only because of the education and training that person has received. There seems to be a direct cause and effect between education and success in life.

For many persons in the United States, education is often perceived as the means to an end: employment. So also can religious education be perceived as the means to an end: eternal life, or "getting to heaven." But it is not quite that simple. There are those who believe that both secular education and religious education should have as their goals much more than pragmatic expectations. As Robert Bellah and his co-authors state so well in *The Good Society* (New York: Alfred A. Knopf, 1991, p. 170): "the idea of an education that simply gives individuals the methods and skills they need to get ahead in the world is almost certainly inadequate, even as 'job preparation,' in an advanced technical economy, which requires morally and socially sensitive people capable of responsible interaction. It is even more inadequate in preparing citizens for active participation in a complex world."

Both secular education and religious education, then, have in the past been mainly concerned with the acquiring of knowledge and skills. These are certainly commendable educational goals, and in the world of curriculum-based programs these goals were achievable by using concrete, predictable methodology. A curriculum based on learning objectives, developmental levels of the students, and measurable outcomes results in an educational model that produces students who are expected to have assimilated the information presented to them. This expectation is present in curriculum-based programs of religious education just as in secular education. In traditional religious education programs, in both Catholic schools and in parish programs, the acquisition of knowledge has been expected and rewarded.

Many Catholics grew up in this learning environment and have turned out to be not only religiously literate but also the faith-filled, committed "Core Catholics" researched and defined by James Castelli and Joseph Gremillion in *The Emerging Parish: The Notre Dame Study of Catholic Life Since Vatican II* (San Francisco: Harper & Row, 1987, pp. 30–52). These "Core Catholics" are those who are "parish-connected," or registered members of parishes, say Castelli and Gremillion, and 48 percent of them participate in parish activities in addition to Mass. They exhibit a variety of opinions concerning the role of the Church in their lives. "About two-thirds of Core Catholics accept church positions on their own terms, often disagreeing with official church teachings. Core Catholics are increasingly affluent and educated. They have absorbed from American culture the values of independence, pluralism, and participatory democracy. They use these values in their work and social lives and see no reason to leave them behind in their religious lives" (p. 51).

Half of Core Catholics attended Catholic grade school, 33 percent attended a Catholic junior high, 28 percent attended a Catholic high school, 13 percent attended a Catholic college, and 23 percent had a family income above $40,000 when this study was done in 1987. It appears that the learning environment from which these Core Catholics emerged did indeed teach them to think reasonably well and to learn skills necessary fo gainful employment.

However, in their foundational beliefs, many Core Catholics seem to be excessively individualistic: 39 percent believe that the Church exists for their own personal salvation. The authors state on page 36: "The large proportion of Catholics with exclusively individualistic foundational beliefs is startling and sobering. This indicates that the church, which emphasizes communal symbols and values, faces constant tension with not only the individualistic impulses of American society, but with similar impulses among large numbers of its own members. To some extent, this impulse toward individualism is the product of four centuries of catechesis which emphasized growth in personal holiness and the individualistic nature of sin, confession, and absolution."

We might want to ask, at this point, just what it is we want to accomplish through our religious educational endeavors. In a curriculum-based program centered on cognitive learning, it seems clear that religious literacy can result in well-educated, affluent Catholics who are capable of thinking for themselves. But many of these same people also appear to be self-centered and perhaps unconcerned with gospel values that insist on reaching out to others in mission and service.

If the goal of all education in today's world can be recognized more in keeping with Robert Bellah's concept in *The Good Society* as that "which requires morally and socially sensitive people capable of responsible interaction," it would necessitate a more comprehensive approach than a cognitive, curriculum-based, traditional classroom model provides.

What would this more comprehensive approach look like? In a catechetical program based on concepts of mission and service, we would want to think of family, of story, of celebration, of community. We would want to gather together all the resources and possibilities open to us. We would not want to be limited to learning situated only in a classroom. We would not want to be constrained by a simply functional view of education. We would, indeed, approach the religious education of our children from every possible perspective. We certainly would not discard the content of a curriculum, but we might want to design that curriculum to provide more opportunities for reflection, for a deepening of the student's awareness of the reality of God's presence in everyday life, and for allowing and encouraging a faith response that takes the form of service.

***TIME OUT!

Before pursuing these ideas further, please take a few minutes to think about the following questions, either alone or with others.

1. What knowledge or information have you gained in the past year that has been of practical value to you? In what ways has it been practical? How have you used that knowledge?

2. What knowledge or information have you gained in the past year that has been of spiritual value to you? How have you grown in compassion, concern for others, or in your own conversion process through this knowledge or information?

3. What is your understanding of the Bellah quotation? How could you restate it to apply to catechesis?

Education Leading to Growth in Faith

Does there need to be a sharp and distinguished break between education that leads to knowledge and education that leads to growth in faith? Is it possible to bring the two to a point of convergence? In previous chapters we have laid the groundwork for an affirmative answer to this question. Catechesis is indeed a process of "educating in faith," as the title of Mary Boys' book so aptly puts it (*Educating in Faith: Maps and Visions,* San Francisco: Harper & Row, 1989). Catechesis accomplishes this "education in faith" by becoming a bridge between the religious tradition and the everyday, ordinary life experiences of those who are a part of the community of faith. Catechesis brings faith into the light of day: catechesis illumines obscure and difficult doctrinal beliefs with the brightness of ordinary experience and transforms knowledge into faith response.

In the emerging world of catechesis, certainty is replaced with searching. Questions emerge when the joys and sorrows of life demand answers. The person grounded in the world of catechesis is not always sure that today's answers will fit tomorrow's questions. In this world, when the child socialized into a religious community grows up, mere membership in that community is insufficient. Indeed, the faith tradition of parents and of the religious community is handed on by means of teaching and example. However, the faith of the emerging adult becomes real and genuine and actually owned through the process of connecting lived experience with the teachings and examples that are a part of the faith tradition. It is almost as if the lived experience brings authenticity to the faith tradition of childhood, and in many cases this is true.

An example from my own life illustrates this. I grew up with parents who, at the time of my mother's death, had been married to each other for over 53 years. My husband grew up with parents who, at the time of his mother's death, had been married to each other for over 49 years. My husband and I were taught, by precept and by example, that marriage is to be viewed as permanent commitment. When we were married at ages 21 and 19, we had not the foggiest notion of what that could mean. But we took it "on faith" that the Church teachings of permanence and commitment in marriage were of value and should be lived out in our own marriage. Our parents modeled these values for us: we were certainly socialized into a tradition of long marriages. But it has taken us many many years of participation in a lifelong commitment for us to come to believe what we were taught. That belief has come out of the experience of a working marriage, with all of the inevitable difficulties associated with two strong-willed personalities, recalcitrant teenagers, serious illness, job loss, relocation adjustments, and numerous ongoing conflicts. That belief has also come out of the experience of a working marriage that has been filled with the inevitable joys of bringing four new lives into the world and nurturing them, of rewarding and meaningful employment, of moments of intense personal closeness, of family celebrations that carry on the traditions that mark and identify us.

Commitment in marriage is a mandate of the Church and a doctrinal teaching that is presented in classrooms in all Catholic religious education programs everywhere. Children learn about this, cognitively, in a formal and intentional manner, in their fifth-grade curriculum which focuses on the seven sacraments. But only in real life, in the experiences that give flesh to the cognitive, do we come to believe in the possibility of commitment in marriage. I believe it now, after all the years of participating in and surviving the joys and sorrows of a long marriage. All the classroom teaching in the world cannot have the same effect: classroom teaching lays the groundwork for the belief that comes from experience.

Integrating Lectionary-Based and Curriculum-Based Catechesis

After all the questions have been asked and after all the theory has been examined, what remains is the task to put it all together into a somewhat workable form. It is time to get real, to look at this time of catechetical transition and discover what is needed to bring together the two worlds of lectionary and curriculum.

There are still many questions which remain unanswered. Do we discard the methods and content of past catechetical efforts because of their apparent ineffectiveness? Or can we retrieve what was good from the past and incorporate it into the contemporary catechetical scene? Can we find a balance between the cognitive learning demanded by a curriculum-based approach and the faith development that is the aim of all catechesis? Is it at all possible to blend or integrate several approaches to catechesis and come up with a synergistic effect that is indeed greater than the sum of its parts? If so, what would it take to accomplish this?

To answer these and other questions surrounding the issues of lectionary-based catechesis, it might be helpful to examine a methodology for catechists that can be used to bring together the best of the two worlds of lectionary and curriculum. In both worlds there are differences of orientation but not always differences in the desired result: growth in faith. The key element in bringing about an effective catechetical experience is, as always, the catechist. Regardless of the orientation of a program, the catechist is the link between content, method, and faith. In bringing together the two worlds of catechesis—lectionary and curriculum—catechists can be most instrumental in adapting the curriculum-based programs into a new environment that includes the lectionary.

Once catechists are convinced of the value of including lectionary readings as part of the content and methodology of the catechetical session, they will do so naturally and almost instinctively. Once catechists are convinced that there is a method for including lectionary readings that works well and that is relatively simple, they will use that method. Once catechists themselves have been formed to be scripturally and liturgically sensitive through a formation experience such as is presented in this book, they will impart that sensitivity to others.

Pastors, parish staff persons and parish catechetical leaders must see the value of the integration of lectionary-based and curriculum-based catechesis. Their support of the catechists is, of course, absolutely vital. This support takes the form of providing opportunities for catechists to study and discuss possibilities for the integration of curriculum-based and lectionary-based catechesis. It is important that catechists are supported in enabling them to participate in formation programs and scripture study groups, making available to them resources of all kinds, and affirming, affirming, and affirming them in all of their efforts to share faith with the children.

Knowing the Content of the Curriculum

The success of the following simple method which enables catechists to integrate lectionary-based and curriculum-based catechesis depends on two things: (1) the familiarity of the catechist with the curriculum and the content of the catechetical materials currently being used in the parish school or catechetical programs, and (2) the familiarity of the catechist with the lectionary readings week by week throughout the year.

The experienced catechist who is thoroughly familiar and comfortable with the content of the catechetical materials currently being used recognizes how those materials correlate with the developmental level of the children being catechized. The less experienced catechist will have to perhaps work harder to reach a certain level of comfort and familiarity with both content of the materials and characteristics of the children, but it is important for the catechist to develop such a comfort and familiarity regardless of the method being used in the catechetical program.

Developing a familiarity with catechetical materials can be a formidable task for catechists in both religious education programs and in Catholic schools. The children's textbooks and teachers' manuals make up only part of the vast array of resources which augment the basic items available to catechists. Additional resources may be obtained that feature music (hymnals, songbooks, tapes and records, instrumental accompaniment), suggestions and ideas for prayer experiences (for children, faculty/catechist/adult gatherings, families), and family activities (home-centered sacramental preparation, teaching guides, seasonal celebrations, prayers). In addition, there are posters, sample parent letters, board games, unit or chapter tests, and classroom management advice. DRE's and school principals need to provide careful guidance for their catechists, lest they become lost forever among all these choices. It is vital, however, that catechists have a working knowledge of and comfort with the basic materials: the children's textbook and the catechist/teacher manual that accompanies it.

In curriculum-based programs, these texts and manuals follow a scope-and-sequence format designed to move progressively throughout the school year. The year is divided into content units, each with its own focus or theme. The units are divided into individual chapters or lessons, each with its own specific topic which expands the focus of the unit. In standard parish religious education programs for children who attend public schools, there are twenty-eight to thirty lessons to be presented, one each week throughout the school year. Materials for parish school religious education programs provide expanded chapters or lessons for use on a daily basis, even though in many schools "religion class" may not be taught on all five days of the week.

The actual content of these units and lessons depends, of course, on the developmental level of the children for whom they are designed. A standard approach to content since the days of catechetical renewal following Vatican II provides for a gradual assimilation of theological knowledge based on the life experience as well as the developmental level of the child. If life experience and developmental levels are respected, the children are capable of making more profound religious or faith connections with what is going on in their lives as they move through their elementary school years.

Good catechetical materials, then, must respect the developmental stages of the children to determine what is presented when and through which kind of experiences. Each year has its own focus, based on what the children are experiencing in their lives and on what the children are capable of understanding. In grade one, the children learn about God the Creator through families that care for them. In grade two, they learn that Jesus is their friend through their increasingly social relationships. In grade three, they learn about Church through the organized structure of their lives. In grade four, they learn morality through their developing sense of right and wrong. In grade five, they learn about the sacraments through their budding understanding of the abstract and of their need to belong. In grade six, they learn about scripture, especially Hebrew scripture, through their new appreciation for historical meaning.

Of course this general plan is not set in concrete, and the order in which the different topics are presented fluctuates among the publishers of various catechetical programs. General topics such as prayer, liturgy, scripture, the Holy Spirit, and some of the sacraments (baptism, penance, eucharist) are repeated and amplified at each grade level throughout the entire curriculum. Reference to grade-level scope-and-sequence charts reveal how the catechetical information builds on what has been presented in the curriculum and prepares for what is to come.

Adolescent catechesis becomes more theologically sophisticated as these themes are reviewed, this time with much emphasis on how the developing human qualities of the young person are part of the journey to a more mature faith. Youth ministry programs add several components to the learning experience: service and social opportunities are offered along with the catechetical dimension. Catechetical materials for adolescent catechesis are bright, trendy, and couched in the current teenage jargon. Because of this format, this material can quickly become as obsolete as yesterday's Top Ten record sales and so publishers often use throw-away newsprint-quality handouts in place of textbooks.

At all grade levels, preferred catechetical materials now contain additional lessons that emphasize a feature of the liturgical year: Advent, Lent, Christmas, Easter, and major feasts and holy days. These additional "Church year" lessons are substituted for a regular unit lesson and thus interrupt the flow of the unit to some degree. The best catechetical materials offer, in addition, a myriad of auxiliary lessons: lessons about the more popular saints and/or contemporary saintly people, lessons concerning "respect for life" or human sexuality, lessons emphasizing specific religious practices and traditions of a variety of cultures and ethnic groups, lessons promoting peace and justice, lessons that teach or review Catholic prayers, devotions, and sacramental rites. The catechist has many options from which to choose in organizing all of this material throughout the school year, and, again, a great deal of guidance is necessary to assist the catechist in maintaining the focus necessary for a cohesive approach on a lesson-to-lesson basis.

***TIME OUT!

Please think about what you have been reading as you consider these questions, and discuss them with another catechist if you wish.

1. In presenting your most recent "religion" or catechetical class, how did you decide what to teach? What materials are primary for you? Which are secondary?

2. How do you prioritize your time in preparing your lessons? How much time do you spend researching the topic you intend to present? How much time do you spend thinking about or praying for or

considering the needs of your students? How much time do you spend assembling materials for activities, writing lesson plans, organizing the classroom?

3. If, because of time constraints, you had to eliminate one of the above planning procedures, which would it be?

4. For you, what is the importance of the liturgical year in deciding what to teach? What is the importance of the Sunday readings in deciding what to teach?

Knowing the Content of the Lectionary

After looking at the preceding section, it is easy to conclude that catechists have more than enough to occupy their time in planning their catechetical sessions without inserting an additional element such as the liturgical year or lectionary readings. However, the opposite can be argued. It is possible to simplify the planning and presentation procedures by recognizing the value of the lectionary readings and by depending on them to provide many of the various options from which catechists can choose in designing their lessons.

We have already mentioned what is necessary for lectionary-based catechesis to become a reality within the context of a real, live catechetical program: the catechist must be familiar with the content of the curriculum-based program and must be equally familiar with the Sunday readings from week to week. All that remains is the catechist's willingness to see connections between both curriculum and lectionary and to make those connections in the catechetical sessions. It sounds ridiculously simple, and yet can have profound impact on the faith life of the children if it is done with care.

All the arguments for lectionary-based catechesis come into play here. The weekly eucharistic celebration forms the very core out of which faith emerges and grows. At Sunday Mass, people of faith gather, praise God, share their lives with each other, and go forth to transform the world with new awareness and new energy. This ideal setting provides an ideal experience that should not be left to disappear into the black hole of everyday life. If the liturgical experience can be recognized as a vital part of everyday life, connecting the reality of human existence with the mystery of faith, it seems obvious that this experience cannot be ignored in our catechetical endeavors.

We want to expand the experience of Sunday to include both preparation before the event and reflection after the event. We want to remember, week by week, what our sacred writings have to tell us about the story of salvation. We want to find ways to emphasize the importance of liturgical celebration, and specifically of the part scripture plays in liturgical celebration, in our catechetical programs. All of this seems quite natural and quite simple in doing lectionary-based catechesis.

The way to bring together the lectionary readings and the content of a curriculum-based program is quite natural and quite simple, too. It only requires that the catechist be willing to *know* what is to be presented from week to week. And this demands that the catechist *knows* what the content of the yearly curriculum is and that the catechist *knows* what the Sunday readings are going to be as the year progresses. All that remains is to put the two together.

In this integrative approach, it will be necessary to discard some traditional ideas about the importance of curriculum-based scope-and-sequence, and to see instead how the liturgical year provides its own scope and sequence. If the concept of Units and Chapters and Lessons can be replaced with the concept of how the lectionary readings connect throughout the seasons of the year, the integration of lectionary and curriculum can be accomplished with ease. Various themes that are developed in any traditional curriculum-based program are also, of course, present in the lectionary readings, and it is possible that these ideas can be taught through recognizing the mutual importance of both the lectionary readings and the traditional program in getting the point across. Each component reinforces the other. The lectionary readings present a scriptural perspective that is amplified in the grade-level lesson, complete with appropriate language, activities, and illustrations that reveal the awareness of what is necessary to respect the developmental level of the child. The grade-level lesson is enhanced by the inclusion of the lectionary readings and the reminder they bring to the children of the Sunday liturgical core experience of family, community, praise, and mission.

This integrative approach to catechesis presents the best of both worlds of curriculum and of lectionary. What begins to emerge is not only a more complete and authentic catechetical experience for the child, but also an opportunity for the catechist to share a more complete and authentic faith. In this integrative approach, a catechist who wishes merely to present the content of the children's text as published in the teacher's manual is challenged to move beyond the curriculum to personal faith and personal expression of faith. When the Sunday scripture readings have importance in the faith life of the catechist, this overflows into the catechetical sessions and into the lives of the students. The catechist soon begins to look at the content of each lesson with new eyes, to see there where the emphasis should be. The catechist does not rely solely on what the authors of the catechetical materials have determined to be important: the catechist looks also to the authors of sacred scripture to discover what is significant and essential. And the catechist puts the two together in presenting concepts that are true expressions of what the catechist has come to know through pedagogical expertise and through scriptural discoveries.

Developing an Integrative-Approach Lesson Plan

After all is said and done, it is in the doing that we actually begin to see how the integration of curriculum-based materials and lectionary readings can be an effective way to catechize. It is time to get practical and to consider just how it might actually work.

So, then, just what would this integrative approach look like? What are the specifics of putting it all together? How does a catechist actually begin to use this approach? Here is a step-by-step method.

1. The catechist studies and becomes thoroughly familiar with the grade-level curriculum-based program to be used throughout the school year. By studying carefully the scope-and-sequence chart and the contents of the children's texts, teacher's manual, and auxiliary materials, the catechist learns what basic themes are addressed in each unit and how the themes are developed in each lesson.

2. The catechist studies and becomes thoroughly familiar with the Sunday readings to be used during each of the liturgical seasons throughout the school year, utilizing as many of the available lectionary-based resources as possible.

3. The catechist then breaks the year into "units" consisting of the liturgical seasons (Ordinary Time, Advent, Christmas, Lent, Easter). Assisted by various resources if necessary, the catechist determines some of the basic themes that emerge during each of these seasons.

4. The catechist then begins to lay out a calendar that matches the schedule of the parish catechetical program, assigning themes to each of the weeks throughout each liturgical season. Many lectionary-based published resources have already done this preliminary theme-development work, and these publications can be very helpful as guides to the catechist.

5. The catechist then consults the grade-level materials and finds there the lessons that present the themes which emerged from the lectionary readings. These lessons are added to the calendar, with matching themes assigned to each week.

6. The catechist now has two sources—lectionary readings and grade-level materials—from which each lesson can be designed.

***TIME OUT!

Please take some time to begin to practice how this process works. Use the following information to develop a sample calendar for the liturgical season of Ordinary Time between Christmas and Lent, Cycle B.

Lectionary Readings and Themes (from the gospels, Sundays of Ordinary Time, Cycle B)

Second Sunday:	(date)	Theme:	God calls us to follow and respond
Third Sunday:	(date)	Theme:	Following God changes our lives
Fourth Sunday:	(date)	Theme:	God is revealed in Jesus
Fifth Sunday:	(date)	Theme:	Jesus cares for the sick and the poor
Sixth Sunday:	(date)	Theme:	Jesus cures lepers and outcasts

Now, using the curriculum-based catechetical materials with which you are most familiar, discover the lessons where these gospel themes are presented or illustrated. List the lessons, matching the dates with the dates of the lectionary readings. The following correlation is based upon the grade four materials from *This Is Our Faith,* Silver Burdett Ginn Religion Division, 1991 school edition.

Grade Four Lessons and Themes

The date for each lesson is determined by the date of the lectionary reading for each of the Sundays of Ordinary Time, Cycle B, as listed above.

(date):	Lesson 8	Theme:	Commandments help us follow Jesus
(date):	Lesson 13	Theme:	Respecting others (7, 10 commandments)
(date):	Lesson 9	Theme:	Worshiping God (1, 2, 3 commandments)
(date):	Lesson 5	Theme:	Beatitudes: caring for others
(date):	Lesson 6	Theme:	Beatitudes: justice

After you have done your own correlation using your own curriculum-based catechetical materials, please consider and discuss the following questions:

1. What were some difficulties you encountered in this practice session? What was easier than you expected?

2. When you looked at the lectionary readings, did you agree with the themes that are presented here? Or did you think of other themes or concepts?

3. What resources (if any) did you use for this exercise?

4. How much time did this practice session take for you to accomplish? What do you see as the value of working ahead in liturgical season "units" rather than week by week?

Now that the preliminary research and calendar work has been accomplished, we come to the easy part. This is where the richness of the integrative approach bears fruit, both for the children and for the catechist's own personal faith and spiritual growth. The actual planning of each lesson becomes a source of encounter with God as the scripture readings are considered in prayerful study. It is out of this experience that the catechist is best able to convey to the students a depth of faith that is lived out in the classroom. This scripture-based lesson, then, comes alive in a new way because the catechist has not only learned the content of what to present but has found in the liturgical celebration surrounding this content other elements that contribute to a lived experience of God's presence at Mass: in presider, assembly, eucharist, *and* in the Word. Because the catechist is part of the assembly who hears the Word and who participates in the sharing of the eucharistic bread and wine, the catechist brings that experience to the catechetical session and uses it as the basis for the lesson. In the integrative approach it is not possible to ignore the liturgical experience or the lectionary readings in catechetical settings. They merge and become equally, mutually important.

Sample Lesson Plan

So what would a sample lesson plan look like? To assist you in working out your own lesson plans, here's an example of a class for fifth graders. This lesson incorporates the format suggested by the children's text with the lectionary readings for the day.

The Third Sunday of Easter, Cycle A

Gospel Reading: Lk 24:13–35 (The Emmaus journey and recognition of Jesus)

Grade 5 Lesson: End of year review of the seven sacraments, from the Grade 5 curriculum.

Students: 24 children (14 boys, 10 girls) in the parish religious education program, grade 5.

Schedule: Sundays, 9:15 a.m. to 10:45 a.m., between parish 8:00 and 11:00 Masses

Format: Classroom setting in nearby local public school which the parish rents for these classes. There is no parish school. Classrooms are cluttered with the usual grade-school paraphernalia and contain table/desks and chairs for the students.

Objectives of the Lesson: To review the seven sacraments as ways to recognize God's presence in our lives, to reinforce the meaning of signs and symbols found in the celebration of the sacraments, and to lead the students to an understanding of why eucharist is the primary experience of God's presence in the lives of Catholic Christians.

Life Experience: Pantomime activity: Students are divided into teams of 4 or 5. Teams choose one person who acts out without words a quality or characteristic that helps to recognize or identify one of the other team members. The rest of the team tries to guess who is being identified.

Reflection: Discussion: How do we come to know another person? What is it that we will always remember about that person even if we don't see him or her for a while? How could we describe that person to another?

Faith Tradition or Message: The catechist relates this activity to the gospel passage for that Sunday, the story of the Emmaus journey and meal found in Luke 24:13–35. A candle is lit, all stand, and after an appropriate sung alleluia the gospel is proclaimed from the lectionary. The catechist guides a homiletic response from the students, asking for their understanding of the meaning of the passage.

The catechist emphasizes how a recognition of God's presence among us is like the disciples' recognition of Jesus when he broke the bread with them. This leads to a brief review of the seven sacraments that have been studied throughout the year and how we recognize God's presence in the signs and symbols of these sacraments. The catechist continues to return to the Emmaus story as an example of how it is possible to bring to mind the presence of someone when we remember a significant event that we experienced with that person. The catechist reviews the sacraments and their signs and symbols again using the Emmaus story as a point of reference.

Reflection and Response: Expanding the theme of signs of God's presence, different kinds of "bread" are displayed for the students: hamburger buns, soda crackers, sweet rolls, plain white bread, dinner rolls, heavy brown bread, cookies, etc. The common element in all of these bread items is wheat or grain, just as the common element in our sacramental life as Catholic Christians is our participation at the table as we encounter Jesus in the bread and wine of eucharist. Another common element in these bread items is found in the Emmaus story: as the friends of Jesus ate with him they recognized him and his importance in their lives, just as we recognize the importance of common bread as bodily nourishment and the importance of eucharist as spiritual nourishment.

Students choose one of these bread items, but before eating they are asked:

Why did you choose the kind of bread you did?

What does your bread have in common with the others?

How is it different?

What effect does eating this bread have?

What if you didn't eat it? Would it matter?

How could you share this bread with someone who was starving?

How does the bread you chose identify for you something good that God has given to you or done for you?

Then the group prays together, with opportunities for prayers of petition for those who are without bread to eat, and ending with prayers of thanksgiving and praise. Finally, the students can eat their chosen bread as they are dismissed.

***TIME OUT!

Now it's your opportunity to plan a catechetical session, based on some of the time-honored principles already presented in this book. First, a review of these principles:

1. Each catechetical session is designed using the catechetical method proposed by Thomas Groome, Robert Hater, and others that begins with a focus on the life experience of the student and an opportunity to reflect on the meaning of that experience. Only then is the faith tradition presented, the doctrinal content or Church teaching that helps to interpret the experience of the student. The next segment of the catechetical sessions encourages the integration of experience with Church teaching with further insight and response ending the session. This methodology reinforces the concept of praxis, which simply means to reflect upon one's experience, that is basic to all catechetical theory. For more about this, see Thomas Groome's original thesis as presented in *Christian Religious Education*, San Francisco: Harper & Row, 1980, especially chapter 9.

2. In all catechetical sessions, the needs of the learners take precedence over the needs of the catechist. Cultural, social, educational, and developmental levels are respected, and material that is used must be appropriate and must reflect the language, pedagogical methodology, sociological situations, and ages of the learners. This means that skill is needed to determine the fine line between challenging and overwhelming the student, between a boring lesson and one which gently persuades, between a productive review session and one that insults the learner's knowledge, and between an experience of God and a meaningless ritual. Constant attention to the students as they grow and change throughout the school year means listening to them, watching them, encouraging their questions, being aware of what goes on in their lives (even if this means going to see "Jurassic Park" or watching some MTV) and joining in their lives in as many ways as is possible.

3. Catechetical theory is useless, of course, without catechists who buy into it. Catechists who are formed in their faith, who are well trained in methodology, and who care deeply about children will devote the time needed to do the job well. Catechist formation programs call out to them, and they respond. Further in-service opportunities fill many of their evenings and Saturdays. Some continue their formal education and enter degree and graduate programs. Others bake cookies to take to class. All catechists who care are filled with love for and from God, and this love shines forth in the classroom and wherever they encounter children. These catechists are the stuff of which saints are made, even as they struggle to remain sane within the crazy world of catechesis. These catechists are indeed "God's chosen ones" as they tend to those smaller versions of "God's chosen ones" in parish schools and religious education programs everywhere.

Basic Lesson Plan Outline

The principles described above are necessary for all catechesis to be done well: (1) having an effective methodology, (2) knowing the needs of the students, (3) and the presence of a faith-filled, informed, and motivated catechist. A fourth element is especially important in lectionary-based catechesis: planning well. Effective lectionary-based catechesis requires a great deal of familiarity with lectionary readings and curriculum-based materials. The successful integration of these two components can best be accomplished when the lessons are thoughtfully planned and organized. Prayerful reflection is needed. Time is spent in thinking out the goals of each lesson based on the scripture themes. There is no way to short-cut the process of planning.

An outline follows that can be used as a guide in your planning. Please use this outline to design a lesson plan integrating the catechetical materials you are most familiar with and the lectionary readings (using the gospel is sufficient) for next Sunday.

Lectionary-Based Lesson Planning Guide

Date of lesson _____

Lectionary reading(s) for this week _____

Theme of lectionary reading(s) _____

Curriculum lesson title and theme _____

My goals or learning objectives: "As a result of this session, I would want the children to be able to _____

_____

_____ "

Life experience: Know what is going on in the lives of the students, and then provide an activity that not only introduces the theme of the lesson but that also relates to what they are doing, what they are familiar with, what is of concern to them. Or an activity can be designed to present a shared expereince for the students, out of which the theme is developed through reflection and further activities. Ask the students: "What are we doing?"

Some ways to develop this segment:
    __ storytelling
    __ personal anecdote
    __ focusing questions, oral or on paper
    __ video, film, tape
    __ newspaper articles, clippings
    __ witness of "guest speaker"
    __ group activity that illustrates the theme of the lesson

Critical Reflection: The students are encouraged to think about the meaning of the "life experience" topic, why it is important to them, and what the likely or intended consequences of this experience might be. Ask the students: "Why do we do what we do?"

Some ways to develop this segment:

___ music
___ journal-writing
___ art activity
___ creative writing activity (poetry, story)
___ discussion in pairs, triads
___ questions and answers

Message of the Faith Tradition: At this point in the lesson it is appropriate to proclaim the lectionary readings in ritual fashion. The readings illustrate and lead to further investigation into the doctrine or faith teachings of the Christian community concerning the theme of the lesson. It is, as always, important to continue to relate to the life experience of the students, with the intention of inviting and encouraging faith response. Ask the students: "What is the teaching of our faith tradition on the topic at hand?"

Some ways to develop this segment:
___ "dialogue homily"-type lecture
___ film, video
___ drama, role playing
___ use of text material

Reflection on or Dialogue Between Life Experience and Faith Tradition: The students again take some time to begin to make connections among the ideas, concepts, and activities that have been presented. By reflecting on the faith tradition as it matches (or challenges!) their own life experiences they are starting to see where change might be indicated or new insight is gained so that the faith response will be authentic. Ask the students: "Now that we understand the topic at hand more clearly, how does or could our life experience reflect our faith tradition?"

Ways to develop this segment:
___ music, art, creative writing
___ journal-writing
___ review of key words, ideas, concepts
___ questioning that challenges
___ problem solving
___ personal witness talks

Faith Response: The students are given the opportunity to make a personal faith response for the future. Their own experiences help them to understand the teaching of the faith tradition and further insight results when the student begins to see those connections. Possibilities for change, conversion, or intended future action are presented. Ask the students: "Now what are we going to do about what we have learned?"

Ways to develop this segment:
— prayer experience
— naming of specific course of action
— art, music, creative writing
— journal writing
— film, video, tape
— text material

Dismissal and blessing.

Using the Lesson Plan Guide

It is obvious in this lesson plan guide that many activities and options are possible in developing each segment. The timing of the catechetical session will limit these options, and it is important that the catechist choose among the activities carefully to present a variety of them week by week. Several activities are certainly appropriate for more than one segment of the lesson: journaling, for instance, could be used often and in many ways. Music and spontaneous or formal prayer might be part of almost every lesson.

The only "activity" that should be in place in each lesson is the proclamation *in ritual form* of the gospel or lectionary readings. It is vital that the scripture portion be *proclaimed* so that it is not to be confused with a fictional story that might be used as an illustration of the children's "life experience" or with stories that are read to them about saints, contemporary heroes, or historical events. Children's textbooks often present nicely illustrated and paraphrased Bible stories. Nice as they are, these stories from the texts should not be used for the lectionary proclamation because the text is not the lectionary. The lectionary should be used for this purpose and the readings should not be paraphrased. Of course the lectionary for children can be considered for proclamation to the younger children and it should be honored in the usual way. Remember that in doing lectionary-based catechesis we are always attempting to bring to mind the parish liturgical experience and that a reenactment of the Liturgy of the Word does not contain paraphrased structure or Bible stories read from the children's text.

A brief word about how Catholic school catechists might want to adapt some of these ideas to the schedule of daily catechetical sessions. The weekly "theme" of the lectionary reading will be incorporated into each daily lesson, but the actual ritual proclamation of the gospel would not, of course, be done each day. In some Catholic schools that are using this model, the lectonary readings and the specific lesson that best illustrates the theme of the readings are presented on Fridays, in preparation for the Sunday parish liturgy. In others, this lesson is done on Mondays, following the Sunday parish liturgy. The "purists" would argue that the fullest impact of the lectionary readings should be during the Liturgy of the Word at the Sunday celebration, and that catechesis is enhanced when the hearers of the Word have had some time to internalize the Sunday experience. Those who are a bit more realistic insist that the children do not retain or remember much about the Sunday readings at Mass, and that including the readings during a portion of the Friday "religion class" helps the children to understand the readings when they do hear them again on Sunday. It is even possible when they hear the readings again on Sunday that the children can relate those readings to the entire catechetical session they experienced in school on Friday. Perhaps both approaches could be combined: a catechetical session on Friday to prepare the children for Sunday's readings, with a reflection/response session on Mondays to both remind them of the parish liturgical experience and to allow them the opportunity to pray God's Word with their classmates. The ultimate goal, however it is accomplished, is to link the parish Sunday liturgical celebrations with the classroom situation.

A Self-Evaluation Process

As catechists we are constantly aware of the impact we may or may not have on the faith of those we teach. Sometimes it is a good thing to take some real time out to evaluate how we ourselves are faring in our own faith life as catechists attempting to share that faith with others. Our expertise as catechists depends not only on the ability to articulate what we have come to believe, but also on how well we are doing with our own deepening faith. This short self-evaluation procedure might be used by catechists to take a look at growth in faith with a new perspective now that some new insight has emerged. In this book we have been considering some ideas such as the relationship between liturgy and catechesis, how scripture can enliven our catechetical endeavors, the importance of scripturally-sensitive catechists, and the ever-constant struggle to maintain catechetical balance between the content of Church teaching and the context of one's experience of God in this life. Perhaps this self-evaluation will further assist catechists in putting it all together.

Self-Evaluation for Catechists

This process should be considered a private one for you. It is suggested that the insight that is gained could be shared with some trusted friends only if you (and they) agree to be totally honest with each other, not to flatter or deny any concerns that might emerge, and of course to maintain absolute confidentiality.

Find a quiet time and place where you won't be disturbed. Look upon this time with yourself as part of your prayer: indeed, God's presence will certainly be with you as you find yourself reflecting on the ways you have attempted to bring God's presence to others. Write if you wish, or just think quietly about the questions. Quiet music might be helpful to sustain a reflective environment for you. Allow as much time as you can, and expect God's peace to be with you.

Think about your last catechetical session with the children in your care. What time of day (or night) was it? Who was there with you? How many children were present? What did the room look like, feel like? What noises were there? Put yourself back into that time and that space and remember.

1. What was my state of mind when I began our catechetical session? Was I relaxed, in control? Was I flustered, or preoccupied with last-minute details?

2. Was I prepared for the session? Did I have all needed materials at hand and in some degree of order?

3. Did I feel that I "owned" the lesson, that I could present the ideas using my own language, my own understanding, my own experience? Did I rely too much on the teaching materials?

4. Did I truly believe what I was teaching? Did the scripture passages make sense to me? Did the church teaching make sense to me? Had I considered both carefully and prayerfully in preparation for the session?

5. How did I respond to the children? Was I delighted with them or did I find myself out of patience? Why?

6. How did the children respond to me? Were they engrossed, focused, absorbed in the session? Did they ask questions? Or were they bored, distracted? Why?

7. What rituals, stories, activities, prayer experiences, or other methods did I use in this session? Which ones seemed to make a difference in the children's responses? Which would I repeat? Which would I not try again?

8. How did the session end? Was the dismissal of the children at the end of the session a real "sending forth" to love and serve God? Or did it end in confusion with projects unfinished or questions unanswered?

9. How present was I to the children after the session? Did I linger for those who needed my personal attention?

10. Was the session, as a whole, an experience of God's presence? Was the session peaceful or was it challenging to the children and to me? Did I fulfill my expectations and goals (both learning and catechetical) in this session? If not, what could I do differently next time?

11. What did I learn in this session about God, Church, my relationships with others? What questions do I still have?

12. What or who keeps me going in my catechetical ministry? Where do I receive guidance, support, affirmation? Who enables me? Do I feel comfortable asking for assistance when I need it?

13. How do I contribute to the guidance, support, affirmation of other catechists, including my pastor, catechetical leader, or principal? How do I enable them?

14. What do I still need to know about what I'm doing as a catechist? What skills need sharpening? What theological understanding is still fuzzy? Am I willing to continue growing in knowledge? How can I do this?

15. What am I most thankful for at this time in my life? How has God blessed me this week, this month, this year? In what ways do I allow God's goodness to fill my heart? How do I respond to all that is good? In what specific ways, this week or this month or this year, can I share God's goodness in mission and service?

Certainly this self-evaluation procedure could be a lengthy one for you, and probably would not be accomplished after each and every catechetical session. However, bits and pieces of it could be considered on a consistent basis. Use it, adapt it for your own needs, redesign it to suit your particular situation. Some sort of evaluation, or reflection on experience, is part of the catechetical process. As catechists we should be willing to include ourselves and our own experiences as being part of that reflection process.

Some Concluding Thoughts

At the conclusion of all these ideas and suggestions, is it realistic to consider the integration of lectionary-based catechesis and curriculum-based catechesis as a viable possibility in parish catechetical programs? Can we state with any true assurance that children will come to a more mature and authentic faith if they experience this combination of catechetical approaches? In short, is it worth the effort?

It is not always possible, of course, to answer with certainty these and other questions about the effectiveness of new ways of handing on the faith. But we do know two things: (1) the Sunday liturgical celebration is absolutely vital to the faith life of the parish community and to the individual members of that community, and (2) catechesis for the parish children, however it is designed or accomplished, is an absolutely vital component of parish life. When these two "absolutely vital" aspects of the faith life of the parish community are separated because of a lack of imagination or interest or even because of historical practice, both are diminished. When these two avenues for the nourishment of faith are brought together, both are enormously enriched.

Catechesis of children must be rooted in the faith life of the parish community. This faith life is evident, lived out, and comes to the fullness of expression when the community gathers to worship. When children experience this communal celebration of the faith, they value the experience, remember it, and are drawn back to it over and over again throughout the years. The liturgical experience has a profound effect on all of us: we can believe the teachings from Vatican II from paragraph 2 of the

Constitution on the Sacred Liturgy that the liturgical celebration ". . . most of all in the divine sacrifice of the eucharist, is the outstanding means whereby the faithful can express in their lives, and manifest to others, the mystery of Christ and the real nature of the true Church." Paragraph 11 says it all: the eucharistic liturgy is indeed "the source and summit of the entire Christian life." We cannot put aside the potential impact of the liturgy on the total catechetical experience of our children.

The other side of the coin reveals what we've been doing to catechize children for generations. We know that when children are catechized in a consistent, systematic and intentional program, they grow in knowledge of the faith tradition. But somehow this knowledge has not always resulted in an owned and mature faith that is capable of living out more fully the gospel message of mission and service, as the Notre Dame study has revealed.

Lectionary-based catechesis presents opportunities for children to be exposed to the gospel message of mission and service through consistent exposure to the Sunday readings, week after week. Curriculum-based catechesis presents opportunities for children to experience the content of the faith tradition through a systematic, intentional, and consistent educational catechetical methodology that respects developmental stages of children. Catechists are the link between the two. Faith-filled catechists who are catechetically and scripturally sensitive are capable of integrating a curriculum with the Sunday readings. Scripturally-formed catechists who have come to value a curriculum-based program of religious education can enhance its value with a simple adaptation that brings the two together. There is considerable potential in this approach and the rewards can be many.

Perhaps the missing element in our past catechetical efforts with children has been the separation of the parish liturgical experience from the parish religious education experience. Perhaps if the two come together through at least the process of linking the lectionary readings with the formal catechetical sessions, the faith of the children will be enhanced. At the very least, the children will certainly recognize the bond that exists within the parish community as they listen together to the Word of God Sunday after Sunday—that same Word of God that the children hear proclaimed week after week in their catechetical sessions. The possibilities are great and the challenge is exciting. Can it be done? We can certainly give it a try.

And finally, one last listing of resources for you:

Bishops of the United States. *Lectionary for Masses with Children*. Chicago: Liturgy Training Publications, 1993.

Bernstein, Eleanor, and Brooks-Leonard, John, eds. *Children in the Assembly of the Church.* Chicago: Liturgy Training Publications, 1992.

Brown, Raymond. *The Critical Meaning of the Bible.* New York: Paulist Press, 1981.

Brown, Raymond. *Responses to 101 Questions on the Bible.* New York: Paulist Press, 1990.

Brown, Raymond, Fitzmyer, Joseph, and Murphy, Roland. *The New Jerome Biblical Commentary.* Englewood Cliffs, NJ: Prentice-Hall, 1990.

Brown, Raymond, Fitzmyer, Joseph, and Murphy, Roland. *The New Jerome Bible Handbook.* Collegeville, MN: The Liturgical Press, 1992.

Coleman, Lyman, ed. *Serendipity New Testament for Groups,* Third Edition. New York: Paulist Press, 1990.

Hamma, Robert M. *The Catechumen's Lectionary.* New York: Paulist Press, 1988.

Halmo, Joan. *Celebrating the Church Year with Young Children.* Collegeville, MN: The Liturgical Press, 1987.

McBrien, Philip. *How To Teach with the Lectionary.* Mystic, CN: Twenty-Third Publications, 1992.

Powell, Karen H., and Sinwell, Joseph. *Breaking Open the Word of God,* Cycles A, B, C. New York: Paulist Press, 1987.

Seasons of Faith Series. Dubuque: Brown Publishing Co., 1990.

Scott, Macrina. *Picking the Right Bible Study Program,* 1992 Edition. ACTA Publications, 1991.

Soulen, Richard N. *Handbook of Biblical Criticism.* Atlanta: John Knox Press, 1978.

Throckmorton, Burton H. *Gospel Parallels,* Fifth Edition. Nashville: Thomas Nelson, Inc., 1992.

Appendix: A Program for Lectionary-Based Catechist Formation

The Faith and Skills of the Catechist

Formation of catechists who will be doing lectionary-based catechesis presents certain challenges not unlike the challenges that are present in all catechist formation programs. As described in the last chapter, it is to be expected that formation of catechists requires that they participate in a gradual process that integrates life experience, information, reflection, and response. Principles of adult learning should of course be respected. It is important that the program be designed to meet the particular needs of the individuals who will be participating. The program should contain aspects of both theory and practice, with an adequate methodology for putting the two together. And it must be practical, useful, and do-able.

In addition to these basics, the particular challenges in forming catechists for lectionary-based catechesis lie specifically in the areas of scripture and liturgy. It is important that the entire formation program be grounded in scripture and in its liturgical use and expression. Therefore, this outline suggests a heavy emphasis on scripture as found in the Sunday readings. In this formation program, catechists who will be integrating lectionary readings into their curriculum-based programs will experience week by week the importance of those Sunday readings as they are incorporated into each session.

The following course outline for a program of lectionary-based catechist formation is a suggestion for one way to prepare catechists for the task of integrating curriculum-based catechesis and lectionary-based catechesis. The outline is divided into two sections, each of which focuses on one aspect of catechist formation.

The first section, "The Faith of the Catechist," contains some of the theoretical and theological background that catechists-learners need to

107

have so that they can hand on the Tradition in an authentic and reliable way. This section consists of eight sessions, each of which follows a format that honors the methodology that should be present in all catechetical endeavors: (1) life experience is explored, (2) Church teaching, as it relates to the life experience, is presented, and (3) reflection and response is encouraged. Catechists-learners experience in these sessions the methodology that they will be using with their students.

The second section, "The Skills of the Catechist," presents a more specific preparation for catechists who will be integrating lectionary-based catechesis and curriculum-based catechesis. They learn how to apply the theory presented in the first section of the formation course, again with special emphasis on biblical and liturgical aspects of catechesis. This section is presented in four sessions, again following the methodology that catechists will be using with their own students.

The course is intended to be presented by facilitators who are qualified because of their expertise and experience to do so. Lecture is at a minimum: group interaction and activities provide participants with opportunities to express what they have learned.

The Faith of the Catechist

Session One: Discovering Scripture

RELATIONAL GOAL: That the catechists-learners begin the process of building community within the learning environment by getting to know one another and the team of facilitators.

LEARNING GOALS: That the catechists-learners discover what they already know about sacred scripture and that they be reinforced and affirmed in that knowledge. That they broaden their understanding of some basic skills and approaches in using scripture-based catechesis.

NAMING LIFE EXPERIENCE: Get acquainted activity: After allowing a few minutes for reflection, participants are invited to introduce themselves and to answer the question: "What is it that you think sets you apart from everyone else in this room? What is it that makes you unique, one-of-a-kind?" Facilitators set the tone by suggesting somewhat impersonal or non-threatening answers of their own. Participants' answers could vary from "I'm the father of triplets," to "I make the best spaghetti sauce in the parish," to "I just completed a 30-day Ignatian Retreat." Facilitators encourage and allow time for interaction, remarks, questions, and polite comments from everyone during this portion of the session. If there is a large number of participants, it might be good to follow the sharing with a refreshment break during which time further socializing can result in further community-building.

NAMING OUR TRADITION: Building on the previous activity, facilitators suggest that we all discover God in different ways because we all come out of unique and differing backgrounds. God is also encountered in our common tradition, however, in a specific way through scripture. The catechists-learners then answer the "Pre-Catechesis Inventory" to assist them in determining what it is they know or don't know about some scriptural basics. This "Pre-Catechesis" activity can be used in several ways: the facilitators could refer to the answers as a guide for establishing the content of future sessions, or the catechists/learners could refer to their answers privately as a point of reference for their own future searchings and questioning.

Some DRE's or catechetical leaders might want to use the "Pre-Catechesis Inventory" in personal interviews or discussions with their catechists, or at a catechist in-service gathering prior to the Catechist Formation program. Obviously, the questions can be modified as needed to suit the individual parish situation.

An informal follow-up discussion of the Pre-Catechesis Inventory questions takes place at this time. If it is apparent that some basic skills such as finding chapter and verse, divisions between OT and NT, or ways to locate specific parts of the Bible need to be taught (or reviewed), now is the time to do that. Comparisons between the lectionary and the Bible can be presented, and some preferred versions of the Bible could be mentioned. Certainly a brief overview of "what the Bible is and what the Bible is not" can be offered. Facilitators should pay particular attention to how the catechists-learners answer the question "What puzzles you most about the Bible?" Ample time for questions and answers is allowed now, and future presentations can be enriched by building on this curiosity or puzzlement.

Following this presentation, catechists-learners might discuss favorite Bible passages or stories in pairs or small groups.

NAMING OUR REFLECTION: The final portion of the Pre-Catechesis Inventory ("How do you experience scripture at this time in your life?") is used as a time for quiet reflection, using a journal or in silence.

NAMING OUR RESPONSE: The gospel from the previous Sunday is proclaimed from the lectionary or the book of gospels in ritual fashion, with the lighting of candles, the book held high during a sung "Alleluia," and all standing. The facilitators introduce a brief dialogue in response to the reading. Group prayer is suggested and led by the facilitators.

FOR THE NEXT SESSION: Listen carefully to the lectionary readings on the forthcoming Sunday. Consider how they speak to you today, at this point in your life. Try to remember key words and phrases from these readings that reveal to you what God could be like. Think about: What is God asking of me in these passages? How could I respond?

Session Two: Discovering God in Scripture

RELATIONAL GOAL: That the catechists-learners discover and strengthen further possibilities for the formation of new friendships and community that began last week.

LEARNING GOALS: That the catechists-learners come to identify and understand their own images of God as formed throughout their lives, and that they realize how the many images of God found in scripture record the ways in which the Israelites and followers of Jesus came to a deepening awareness of the nature of God.

NAMING LIFE EXPERIENCE: Catechists-learners are asked to re-introduce another person to the group, mentioning what they remember of the unique or unusual quality or experience of that other person. Group mingling is allowed for a few minutes for some reacquainting before the introductions occur.

NAMING OUR TRADITION: Facilitators utilize the previous activity to reinforce the concept of knowing God through scripture. Just as we come to know each other more deeply through repeated encounters, we also come to know God in many ways, in different circumstances and through the various people, places, and experiences of our lives. Scripture is full of stories about these encounters with God that reveal what God is like. The facilitators may offer a brief presentation about images of God in Hebrew scripture, with emphasis on ways in which the "names" for God that occur reflect the experience of the people. Introduction of some biblical themes (creation, covenant) would be appropriate at this time. A scripture-search activity with chapter and verse references to some "names" of God or some biblical themes provides an opportunity for the catechists-learners to practice their "Bible skills" at this time.

NAMING OUR REFLECTION: In quiet reflection, using journals or silence, catechists-learners answer the questions "Where have my images of God come from? What images of God did I bring here with me to this gathering? What new images might I take home with me when I leave?"

NAMING OUR RESPONSE: Again, the gospel reading for the previous Sunday is proclaimed in ritual fashion, with candles, song, lectionary or book of gospels, and everyone standing. Again, reflection on the

113

readings is given by the facilitators and there is an opportunity for all to engage in dialogue. Prayer based on the readings is open to spontaneous response.

FOR THE NEXT SESSION: Listen carefully to the Sunday lectionary readings this week at Mass. See if you can pick out key words or phrases that identify a particular "image" of God for you that might be new or unexpected. Ask: "How is God portrayed in these readings? Is this the way I would expect God to be? What new insight into the nature of God do these passages provide for me this week? How might I respond?"

Session Three: Discovering Jesus in the Gospels

RELATIONAL GOALS: That catechists-learners continue the formation of friendships and the building of community, and that they begin to discover ways to expand these friendships to include families and other parishioners.

LEARNING GOALS: That catechists-learners come to a more profound understanding of the identity of Jesus as both human and divine through investigation into the gospel stories, and that they begin to find new ways to live out the gospel message found in the life, death, and resurrection of Jesus.

NAMING LIFE EXPERIENCE: In silence, catechists-learners write some of their own biographical information in booklet form titled with the date and "The Gospel According to (name)."

Please fill in the blanks honestly and with care. There are no wrong answers!
1. The place where I was born is _____.
2. My occupation is _____.
3. This is a picture of something important to me.
4. Three things I would do if someone gave me a week off with unlimited funds and no responsibilities:
    1.
    2.
    3.
5. This is my first reaction when
    1. I become angry:
    2. I lose something important:
    3. I am hurt by someone I love:
6. Here is a word or phrase that describes the way I feel about
    1. God:
    2. Other people:
    3. Myself:
7. The greatest joy in my life has been _____.

Catechists-learners then silently exchange these booklets with one other person. After each quietly reads the biographical information of the other person, they begin to discuss the last statement. This can lead into further discussion of the previous material if they desire. It is probable that a more personal level of sharing will occur as they share stories about their families, friendships, and feelings. Facilitators will allow ample time for this activity to progress, especially during the discussion period.

NAMING OUR TRADITION: Facilitators will make the obvious connection between written biographical materials and human communication: limitations and advantages of both means of coming to know another person. In scripture there are similar connections as we come to know Jesus through the written accounts of his life, death, and resurrection and through the people who live out the gospel message in their lives today. Various "images" or titles of Jesus in scripture are used to enable an understanding of the human and divine nature of Emmanuel, God with us. Some brief remarks are made concerning the struggles of the early Church councils (Nicea, Constantinople, Ephesus, Chalcedon) to "name" Jesus as both human and divine.

NAMING OUR REFLECTION: Catechists-learners are given a selection of pictures of Jesus (copies of classic and modern paintings, sculptures, mosaics, frescoes, from many ages and many cultures) to contemplate. In silence, they are asked to consider how these images speak to them of their perception of the nature of Jesus: as reconciler, friend, healer, God, risen and glorified, suffering servant, miracle worker, teacher, etc. Journal writing or quiet meditation follows.

NAMING OUR RESPONSE: The gospel from the previous Sunday is proclaimed in ritual fashion as in earlier sessions, with dialogue following. Participants are requested to voice the prayers that follow using an "image" of Jesus that enables them to bring to life the gospel passage they have just heard proclaimed.

FOR THE NEXT SESSION: Again, catechists-learners are encouraged to listen carefully to the lectionary readings for the forthcoming Sunday, attempting to find in them ways in which God is calling them to live out their faith in the place where they find themselves at this time: family, parish, neighborhood, workplace, or proximate or global community.

Session Four: Discovering a Sacramental Church

RELATIONAL GOAL: That catechists-learners will begin to stretch beyond the personal friendships established at these gatherings to consider the inclusion into their circle of concern those whom they don't yet know or understand, with special emphasis on who they perceive "church" to be.

LEARNING GOALS: That catechists-learners will understand more clearly some ways in which the church ritualizes and brings to life the experience of God through sacramental encounter, and that they will recognize the sacramental relationship between Word and eucharist.

NAMING LIFE EXPERIENCE: Catechists-learners answer, first on paper and then in small groups, the questions: "What was my experience of Church when I was ten years old? What do I remember? What is my experience of Church today? What would I like to keep from the past? What would I like to discard?"

NAMING OUR TRADITION: Facilitators encourage large group response to the previous questions, and lead into a short presentation comparing some various ecclesiologies from the past (Church as persecuted community, as institution, as authority) with a contemporary understanding of Church as people of God. This broader concept of "Church" carries with it the responsibility to accept those whose encounters with God may be expressed in different ways and at different times, and this is especially evident in scripture.

Out of this concept of Church emerges an understanding of sacrament that speaks of encounter with God, of celebrating and ritualizing within the faith community the encounter and resulting conversion, commitment, or response which is in process or which has already taken place. A brief overview of "the seven" is given, emphasizing the "encounter" aspect of each sacrament. The particulars of the rites and liturgical celebrations of the sacraments will be covered at a later session. At this time it is important to establish the groundwork for mutual understanding of the nature of sacrament and to make connections between sacramental encounter and encounter with God in scripture. The equality and similarity of God's presence in both Word and eucharist is emphasized, and the relationship between the presence of God found within the worshiping community and in the one who presides at liturgy is also brought out. The experience of God in Word, eucharist, community, and leader of the community is described as mutually expressive of the sacramental encounter.

117

NAMING OUR REFLECTION: In silent reflection or with their journals, catechists-learners consider the question asked of those candidates for initiation as they celebrate the Rite of Entrance into the Order of Catechumens: "What do you ask of God's Church?" Catechists-learners then reflect upon their response to a related question: "What does the Church ask of me?"

NAMING OUR RESPONSE: The previous Sunday readings are proclaimed as before. Participants respond in dialogue fashion, and prayer is spontaneous. Because the facilitators have been modeling this ritual well, by now catechists-learners should be fairly comfortable with the format. They can be encouraged and expected to participate quite willingly in doing the readings, leading the prayers, and performing other parts of the ritual.

FOR THE NEXT SESSION: The catechists-learners again listen to and consider the forthcoming Sunday readings with care and prayer, finding within them some indications of what it is God is asking or calling for in their lives.

Session Five: Discovering Scripture and Liturgy

RELATIONAL GOAL: That catechists-learners continue the process of finding ways to reach out to others outside of their immediate circles of friendship to expand the reign of God. The theme of mission and service begins to be an integral part of these sessions, implicit in all that is presented by the facilitators.

LEARNING GOALS: That catechists-learners understand more fully the meaning of the rites, rituals, and liturgical celebration of the sacraments, and especially the role scripture plays in these celebrations.

NAMING OUR EXPERIENCE: Facilitators briefly explain and describe the meaning of religious sign and symbol: a sign gives or provides information, while a symbol expresses or represents that which is not clearly understood, and points to something that has a deeper and more profound meaning than what appears on the surface. Some examples: a McDonald's sign informs us that food is instantly at hand. It can also be understood as a symbol of American entrepreneurial success. My wedding ring is a sign that informs others that I am married. However, the ring can also be understood as a symbol of my commitment and fidelity to my husband and to Christian marriage.

Following this brief explanation, catechists-learners are asked to design symbols (using art materials, music, poetry or words) that express one of these key moments in their lives: birth, death, commitment, forgiveness, healing, or sharing a celebratory meal. Emphasis should not be on "churchy" symbols such as the ones usually associated with these experiences, but rather they are encouraged to express these events using contemporary, relevant symbols. Creative efforts are then shared with all.

NAMING OUR TRADITION: Facilitators present a brief overview of the rites and rituals surrounding the celebrations of sacraments. Emphasis here should be on commonalities that exist among the various rites: the use of gestures, visible and dramatic signs, the significance of the presence of the community, the reasons for celebrating these sacramental rituals within the context of eucharistic liturgy, the insistence upon lavish and enthusiastic symbols, and so on. The use of scripture in the rites should be particularly emphasized, not only as scripture is proclaimed within the eucharistic liturgy that surrounds the celebration of the rites, but also ways in which scripture enhances the specific understanding of the presence of God in our midst during these sacramental encounters.

119

NAMING OUR REFLECTION: Catechists-learners again prayerfully reflect in silence or with their journals as they consider the question: "How can I be 'sacrament'—a sign or symbol of God's loving presence—to others?"

NAMING OUR RESPONSE: The lectionary readings from the previous Sunday are once again proclaimed and followed by dialogue and prayer. The catechists-learners are challenged to discover in these readings additional insight into the understanding of "sacrament" in the Church as well as in everyday life.

FOR THE NEXT SESSION: Catechists-learners listen with care to the lectionary readings for the forthcoming Sunday, and attempt to find there God's call to holiness and the moral life. Ask: "Is there a hint in these readings that would help me discern right from wrong? What is the message in these readings that could assist me in my attempts to do good and avoid evil?"

Session Six: Discovering Scripture and Morality

RELATIONAL GOAL: That catechists-learners come to understand and accept a person-centered morality more than an act-centered morality as they live out their lives in mission and service.

LEARNING GOALS: That catechists-learners discover a scriptural view of morality that is motivated by loving service more than by only obeying rules that govern behavior.

NAMING LIFE EXPERIENCE: In small groups, catechists-learners consider the following questions: "When you were growing up, who told you what was right or wrong? How did they convince you of what was right or wrong? Today, who tells you what is right or wrong? What methods are used today to convince you?"

NAMING OUR TRADITION: Building on answers to these questions, the facilitator's presentation focuses on a contemporary understanding of morality that takes a relational rather than act-centered approach. The scriptural foundation for this approach can begin with an examination of the decalogue and the advantages and disadvantages of law as a basis for morality. The message of the Hebrew prophets and their insistence on fidelity to the covenant leads into the perfection of the law and the new covenant that is found in the life and moral teachings of Jesus. The Beatitudes in the gospels of Matthew (Ch. 5) and Luke (Ch. 6) show clearly how the teachings of Jesus do not abolish the law but rather fulfill it, and indeed make stronger demands for perfection than does adherence to the law.

A developmental approach to contemporary morality can also be presented at this time, citing stages of moral development as researched by Lawrence Kohlberg and Carol Gilligan and the ways these stages fit into the progress from rule-centered morality (ten commandments) to societal morality (the prophets) to a principled and self-sacrificing morality (Jesus) that is found in biblical teachings. Brief remarks about how all of this affects conscience formation can end the presentation.

NAMING OUR REFLECTION: With journals or in quiet reflection, catechists-learners ask themselves: "How do I see the connection between service to others and fidelity to God's call? What happens in our lives, families, relationships, communities, society when we fall short of this ideal?"

NAMING OUR RESPONSE: The lectionary readings from the previous Sunday are ritually proclaimed, discussed, and prayed as usual. Catechists-learners are urged to consider these readings to discover how their own "moral stance" might be challenged by the gospel message.

FOR THE NEXT SESSION: The catechists-learners are asked to listen carefully to the lectionary readings for the forthcoming Sunday to discern within them the continuing call to peace, justice, and conversion. Ask: "In these readings, how do we come to understand the nature of the reign of God? How can we be a part of bringing about the reign of God?"

Session Seven: Discovering the Scriptural Call to Justice

RELATIONAL GOAL: That catechists-learners deepen their understanding of morality based on personal relationship to a concept that includes a broader morality that fosters peace and justice to all God's people.

LEARNING GOALS: That catechists-learners understand the scriptural concept of the "reign of God" to mean the participation in attempts to do what is possible to bring about a world of peace, justice, love, joy, and fulfillment, and that they realize that all catechetical efforts should be aimed at this ultimate goal.

NAMING LIFE EXPERIENCE: Catechists-learners look for examples of oppression, injustice, poverty, and other evidence of societal wrongs as they examine newspapers, news magazines, and remember what they might have seen and heard on radio and television. In small groups, then in large group response, these examples are discussed with these questions in mind: "Have I/we (the Church) contributed to this injustice in any way? What could I/we begin to do to address this injustice? What does official Church teaching have to say about this? What does scripture have to say about this?"

NAMING OUR TRADITION: Facilitators attempt to bring together connections between scriptural calls to bring about the reign of God (peace, love, justice) as found in the consistent gospel message and the ways the Church has attempted to address these issues through its teachings on social justice. The communal nature of sin might also be discussed at this time.

NAMING OUR REFLECTION: In journals or in silent reflection, catchists-learners consider: "What are some specific ways that I can promote peace in my family? in my community? in the world? What specific things might I begin to do this week to participate more fully in my attempts to bring about God's reign?"

NAMING OUR RESPONSE: The lectionary readings from the previous Sunday are proclaimed as in past sessions. The usual response is elicited, with particular attention beting paid to how these readings speak to us of peace, justice, and God's love.

123

FOR THE NEXT SESSION: Catechists-learners once again listen to lectionary readings from the forthcoming Sunday. In them, they attempt to find messages of hope, consolation, and peace. Ask: "What is God saying to me in these readings about ways to love each other? What is the scriptural message of hope in these passages?"

Session Eight: Discovering Liturgical Catechesis

RELATIONAL GOALS: That the friendships that have begun in these sessions model for the catechists-learners what God's love can be like, and that these friendships can be extended to include others wherever they find themselves.

LEARNING GOALS: That the virtue of hope can be understood within the context of all liturgical celebration, and that catechists-learners will begin to recognize lectionary-based catechesis as an important part of how they bring the gospel message to those they catechize.

NAMING LIFE EXPERIENCE: Catechists-learners are given copies of the lectionary readings for the forthcoming Sunday. In small groups they are asked to design a prayer experience based on these readings that would be appropriate for use by those they catechize. Components of the prayer experience can include: gathering prayer, readings, psalm response, individual prayers of petition, thanksgiving, praise, or forgiveness, meditative response with music or silence, group prayer, blessings, and prayer of sending.

NAMING OUR TRADITION: A presentation by the facilitators emphasizes the role of liturgical celebration in doing catechesis: that liturgy is not meant to catechize directly nor is catechesis meant to be a direct form of liturgy, but that the two are intimately related within the faith life of the community. Catechesis, which elicits a deepening of faith, prepares us for liturgy as we learn about the structure, intent, and components of the liturgical celebration. Catechesis, a deepening of faith, is also experienced during the liturgy as we come to know more profoundly the nature of God and of God's call. Catechesis, calling forth a faith response, is finally experienced following the liturgy as we reflect on the experience of the Word, of prayer, and of community.

NAMING OUR REFLECTION: The small groups of catechists-learners consider and share with each other ways in which the prayer experience they designed expresses their own hope in the goodness of God and their response to God's goodness.

NAMING OUR RESPONSE: The participants celebrate one of the prayer experiences designed during this session. The participants then celebrate the end of this series of sessions by sharing a pot-luck meal, wine and cheese, dessert and coffee, or whatever seems appropriate.

The Skills of the Catechist

These four practical sessions should follow the eight catechetical sessions that were presented in "The Faith of Catechists." In these sessions, catechists are given the opportunity to learn new skills, to increase their understanding of scripture, and to find ways to put to use what they have learned and experienced in the previous sessions.

There is no question that catechetical skills are important. However, this section of the lectionary-based catechist formation program does not cover classroom management, discipline techniques, or developmental characteristics of children. If catechists are in need of this information, they should and must be presented in another course at another time.

In these sessions the emphasis is on enabling catechists to move into a scripture or lectionary-based approach, with the ultimate goal of preparing them to integrate lectionary-based catechesis and curriculum-based catechesis. The four sessions are designed to follow the same format as the previous section, again with emphasis on group participation and with the expectation that catechists will see modeled in this sessions the methodology that they would use with their students.

Session One: Connecting Scripture and Catechesis

RELATIONAL GOALS: That those attending these sessions continue building and sustaining the friendships they began in the previous sessions, and that they indeed recognize each other now as "catechists" who are seeking to mature and grow in their own faith while discovering new ways to share and express that faith.

LEARNING GOALS: That those attending these sessions understand more profoundly the meaning of their identity as "catechists," that they learn some of the many ways faith can be expressed within the context of catechesis, and that they begin to recognize that scriptural or lectionary-based catechesis requires its own particular methodology and skills.

NAMING LIFE EXPERIENCE: Catechists and the team of facilitators renew friendships begun in the previous sessions and become acquainted with new participants. A "catch-up" discussion is led by the facilitators, and everyone is given the opportunity to speak briefly about experiences, events, new insights, and so on that have occurred since the last gathering. Emphasis here is not only on personal news, but should expand to include some aspect of growth in faith and/or understanding.

NAMING OUR MESSAGE: Building on comments from the previous segment, facilitators make connections to catechetical theory: life experience undergirds all that we do as catechists. Definitions of "catechesis" are presented, with references to the National Catechetical Directory, the Catechism of the Catholic Church, and other pertinent documents. Various approaches to catechesis (developmental, socialization, indoctrination, behavioral, initiatory, and experiential) are discussed. The emphasis here is on the difference between catechesis and the teaching of religion and between catechists and teachers who are involved in other educational endeavors. The tie-in with scriptural catechesis is presented: a background in catechetical theory is important in order to avoid any tendencies toward fundamentalism.

NAMING OUR REFLECTION: In small groups, catechists discuss with each other what they have just heard, restating in their own words a definition for "catechesis" and for "catechist."

NAMING OUR ACTION: In their small groups, catechists design a tee-shirt slogan or an advertising campaign that promotes the ministry of catechesis: "Catechists do it with faith" or "Join the catechetical team and see the world expand" or similar ideas. These slogans are shared with the entire group and can be used to adorn the gathering place for the duration of the sessions.

NAMING OUR RESPONSE: As in the "Faith" sessions, catechists once again participate in lectionary-based catechesis and prayer. The readings from the previous Sunday are proclaimed in ritual fashion, a dialogue "homily/discussion" follows, and it concludes with spontaneous prayer.

FOR THE NEXT SESSION: Catechists are asked to listen carefully and prayerfully to the lectionary readings on the forthcoming Sunday and to attempt to discover in them some answers to the following questions:
   1. What do I find difficult to understand in these readings?
   2. What is clear to me?
   3. What could be the religious meaning or significance to the scripture story I have just heard?
   4. In these readings, what is God asking me to do? to give up? to change? to forgive? to accept?

Session Two: Connecting Scripture and Personal Interpretation

RELATIONAL GOALS: That as the catechists share with each other their own concerns and fears relating to personal interpretation of scripture they will discover they are not alone in these feelings of inadequacy. Together they can begin to build confidence in their abilities to interpret wisely as exegetical skills are developed.

LEARNING GOALS: That the catechists/learners recognize the importance of exegesis in coming to a personal response to scripture.

NAMING LIFE EXPERIENCE: Individually, then in small groups, catechists/learners consider the question: "How can I trust my own understandings of what I read or hear in scripture? How do I know I'm 'right' in my interpretation?" Doubts and fears are allowed to surface in large group response.

NAMING OUR MESSAGE: Facilitators present some practical information about the gospels to the catechists: when the four gospels were written, who the authors might be, something about the various communities for whom the gospels were written and why, the formation of the gospels out of the original oral proclamation, the literary genre (parables, narratives, poetry), the historical background, references to Hebrew scripture, and so on. The following format for doing exegesis is presented to assist the catechists in their own scripture research.

Process for Exegesis

Catechists/learners are given copies of the lectionary readings for the forthcoming Sunday. Various commentaries, scripture study materials, and other resources are made available to them for consultation. They are asked to work together in small groups to answer these questions about the gospel reading:

1. When was this written? by whom? for whom?

2. What were the problems, situations, or concerns of the Christian community when this passage was written?

3. What message did the passage intend to convey when it was written?

131

4. What is clear in this passage? What is unclear? What might you think is the obvious meaning of the passage? What might you have further questions about?

5. What is the immediate context of this passage? What comes immediately before and immediately after it? What is its relationship to the whole gospel?

6. What are some of the text use problems? Can you identify the literary genre, historical significance, function of the text within the community for which it was written?

7. How does God speak through this text to the Church and to me today?

8. How does this text fit within the liturgical year? Why is it used at this time?

9. What does God speaking through this text ask of me? of my Church? How might I/we respond?

This procedure for exegesis is briefly explained by the facilitators, and time is allowed for questions and discussion surrounding the need for exegesis when scripture is used as a basis for catechesis. Concerns about a fundamentalist approach to scripture are discussed, and the facilitators present a brief overview of the ways form, historical, and redaction criticism are used in understanding scripture.

Facilitators can expect frustration from the group of catechists/ learners as they attempt this process of exegesis, especially if they are new at this. There is a great temptation to skip directly to Step 8 when reading/studying/praying scripture. It is hoped that catechists/learners who will be doing lectionary-based catechesis will also recognize the importance of arriving at Step 8 through a more thorough investigation into sources other than one's own intuition or experience, and to rely on the insight and scholarship of linguistics, archaeology, and scriptural scholarship in general to assist in a deeper and more profound understanding of God's word in our lives. It might be said that the Word of God can reach its fullest potential for faith and spiritual growth within the context of the exegetical process.

NAMING OUR ACTION: Catechists are introduced to various biblical commentaries, scripture study programs, copies of some pertinent articles, a complete bibliography, and any other materials that seem relevant. The facilitators offer a "hands-on" activity so that catechists can examine all these materials as thoroughly as possible. Plenty of time will be needed for this: the idea is to expose catechists to the myriad resources available for scripture study and to allow them the opportunity to discover what might be helpful for them and what might entice them to further study, research, and even spiritual growth.

NAMING OUR REFLECTION: In journals or in silent reflection, catechists answer a question based on number 7 in the procedure for exegesis, with the modification: "How does God speak through scripture to the Church and to me today?" This is an ongoing question with which catechists will be struggling continuously, and it is hoped that they will discover that when an exegetical approach is used, the answers to this question are indeed authentic and true to the Christian faith tradition that is handed on by our Church.

NAMING OUR RESPONSE: The lectionary readings from the previous Sunday are proclaimed as before, and discussion and prayer are included.

FOR THE NEXT SESSION: Catechists are asked to consider the lectionary readings from the forthcoming Sunday in a deep and prayerful fashion. They will be using these readings for an extensive practical session next time, during which they will be preparing an actual exegesis of the gospel passage.

Session Three: Connecting Scripture and Tradition

RELATIONAL GOAL: That the catechisits recognize that as members of this learning community they are called to reach out to catechize others, to spread the "good news" in as genuine and authentic a way as possible.

LEARNING GOALS: That the catechists come to know and believe in the necessity of scholarship and exegesis in coming to a deeper and more authentic understanding of scripture, and that they understand that the message they proclaim must be based on a solid core of faith tradition rather than only on a fundamentalist or personal interpretation of what they intuit or sense.

NAMING LIFE EXPERIENCE: Catechists read silently a short passage from a contemporary novel or short story such as this section from the Epilogue of Jane Smiley's novel *A Thousand Acres*. This metaphor for the tragic end of one "normal" family describes the disintegration of the American farmer and the way of life that farm families experienced in the past:

> The Boone Brothers Auction House was plenty busy that spring, and for years to come, riding on the surging waves of the land as it rolled and shifted from farmer to farmer. I wasn't told where our dishes and our couches and our tractors and our pictures and our frying pans washed up. Our thousand acres seems to have gone to The Heartland Corporation, which may or may not have had some of the Stanleys in it—perhaps some of the Stanley cousins who'd long ago moved to Chicago. The Chelsea, that once came on a train, was too big to move, so they bulldozed it. Rose's bungalow went to Henry Grove, as it had once come from Columbus, and my house, too, was taken down to make room for an expansion of the hog buildings to give them a five-thousand-sow capacity. When you stand at the intersection of County 686 and Cabot Street Road now, you see that the fields make no room for houses or barnyards or people. No lives are lived any more within the horizon of your gaze (p. 368).

Catechists discuss the passage in small groups, looking for personal meaning and significance, and then more deeply to discover how some kind of historical or universal knowledge of the issue of closing down family farms because of financial hardship could affect one's personal understanding of the cited passage. The facilitators encourage response from the entire group, emphasizing that some of the aspects of exegesis (examining the historical perspective, the literary genre, the audience, the Bible as art, one's personal experience) assist in an authentic interpretation of this fictional passage.

NAMING OUR TRADITION: The facilitators then briefly review the process of exegesis as described in the previous session. Working alone or in pairs, catechists are asked to apply this process to the gospel passage from the previous Sunday, choosing among the scripture commentaries and resources that have been made available.

NAMING OUR REFLECTION: In pairs or small groups, catechists are asked to share their insight into the gospel passage they have been studying.

NAMING OUR RESPONSE: Instead of the gospel proclamation for the forthcoming Sunday as in the past, the gospel reading that was used in this session for exegesis and study is the basis of prayer response. The homiletic response in dialogue should reflect a deepened understanding of the passage, but facilitators should take care to allow and encourage real prayer to be expressed by the participants, emphasizing that the desired response to scripture (caring and serving others) begins in prayer.

FOR THE NEXT SESSION: Catechists listen carefully and prayerfully to the readings for the forthcoming Sunday, and at some time later in the week prepare another written exegesis of those readings. This exegesis will be the basis for preparing a lesson plan based on an integration of the scripture passage with a "regular" lesson that might be found in a curriculum-based religious education program for children.

Session Four: Connecting Lectionary and Curriculum

RELATIONAL GOAL: That catechists will end these sessions with friendships and networking possibilities that will be carried on into future ministry.

LEARNING GOAL: That catechists will learn how to design a lesson-planning procedure that allows and encourages an integration of the Sunday lectionary readings with a traditional curriculum-based lesson.

NAMING LIFE EXPERIENCE: In pairs, catechists are asked to refer to the exegesis they prepared of the gospel reading from the previous Sunday. They look for themes within the gospel that might connect with a theme in the curriculum-based teacher's guides and children's text.

NAMING OUR TRADITION: In the same pairs, catechists examine their teacher's guides for a lesson that connects with the theme of the gospel reading. They note the methods presented by the textbook authors to encourage comprehension and faith response. Facilitators then suggest a methodology that will enable the gospel reading and the curriculum-based material to come together, presenting principles for the integration of lectionary-based catechesis and curriculum-based catechesis found in Chapter 5 of this book. Briefly outlined, these principles and procedures to accomplish them are:

1. In preparation for planning the catechetical session, the catechist prayerfully considers the Sunday lectionary readings that will precede the session. After reading all three passages several times, the catechist begins to focus on the gospel and works out a simple exegesis using commentaries and other resources.

2. When the catechist becomes aware of several themes that begin to emerge from the gospel, the teacher's guide is consulted to determine how these scriptural themes can be incorporated into the lesson that is being planned.

3. The lesson in the teacher's guide becomes the model for activities that will enhance understanding of the theme to be presented. The content of the lesson is expressed in the gospel reading, and the catechist continuously refers to the gospel message as the lesson progresses.

The catechists then design a lesson plan based on these principles and concepts, connecting their exegesis of the Sunday gospel reading with a lesson in their teacher's guide. It is not necessary that these lesson plans be completed in this session, but rather that a methodology is presented that will allow the catechists to continue the process.

NAMING OUR REFLECTION: A question-and-answer period follows the previous process. For this session it would be good to have on hand a number of experienced catechist/facilitators who could give individual assistance to those working on their lesson plans.

NAMING OUR RESPONSE: The closing prayer experience for these sessions is based, as always, on the lectionary readings for the previous Sunday. At this last session, participants are asked to incorporate prayers of thanksgiving and praise for the friendships that have developed, naming specific people and their individual gifts. Following the prayer, a pot luck dessert, lunch, or late supper could celebrate the completion of the catechist formation series. A roster of names, addresses, and phone numbers should be made available for those who wish to be included on the list: facilitators need to be aware that some people do not wish to have that information made public. This roster, however, gives all the participants the opportunity to keep in touch and network as they continue their spiritual journey through lectionary-based catechesis.